How to be a Real Estate Investor

Discover how you can make
fast cash and
build wealth
investing in real estate

By
Phil Pustejovsky

ISBN-13: 978-1475235210
ISBN-10: 1475235216

DISCLAIMER: This publication is for informational purposes only. Please consult qualified attorneys, accountants and other professionals regarding business and investment decisions.

This book is dedicated to anyone who has ever dreamed big.
You are capable of far more than you could ever imagine.

Contents

Introduction

While bored out of my mind, sitting behind a desk one day, I considered how to be a real estate investor. I was fresh out of college with a degree in mechanical engineering from Vanderbilt University. Many well intentioned adults tried to convince me that the American dream was to get a 9 to 5 job with a Fortune 500 company. But, it sure didn't feel that way once I got one! I was falling asleep at my desk and had no freedom. It quickly dawned on me that I didn't want this for the rest of my working life. In fact, it was about that time that I heard someone refer to the word "job" as an acronym standing for, "Just Over Broke." I wanted the exact opposite. I wanted to be financially free.

I began researching how to become financially free at the library and at book stores. Real estate investing surfaced as a common thread amongst many economically successful people that I studied. That's when I began to consider how to be a real estate investor. What fascinated me about real estate was that there were techniques for making money that didn't require investing cash or using my credit, which was perfect for me at that time because I didn't have any money or any credit.

I devoured every book I could get my hands on and attended free tele-seminars, webinars and local live seminars. A whole new exciting world was opening up to me and it appeared to be exactly what I was looking for. It was a way to become financially free. Before I could begin to truly educate myself on the subject, however, my boss and I had a disagreement at work one day that led to me quitting my Fortune 500 job.

Rather than go get another job, I decided to focus my full time efforts on real estate. It was quite a gamble considering I had very little money saved up, no money coming in, and no experience in the field. But, I was determined to make it work. My parents weren't all that pleased with my decision because they had just spent a substantial amount of money on my college education. They reasoned that I didn't need to go to one of the most expensive colleges in America to be a real estate investor. They recommended I get a job and do real estate on the side until my real estate endeavors were paying me more than my job. It was sound advice that went through one ear and out the other.

The books and seminars made real estate investing sound so easy. I thought to myself, "If I have all day, every day, to devote to real estate, how hard can it be?" In hindsight, that one thought was a major miscalculation. I had failed to consider the fact that I absolutely did not know what I was doing. Real estate, as I discovered, is a business that has tremendous potential, but you really have to know what you're doing to be successful with it. At the time, I didn't have any money to invest in my education, so unfortunately, I was learning every important lesson of real estate the hard way...through the school of hard knocks.

I burned through my savings. Because I had no money coming in, I couldn't pay my bills. When I couldn't pay my rent, I literally went homeless. I was forced to live out of my truck. Some have asked me why I didn't move back in with my parents when this happened. Maybe it was pride, or stubbornness or embarrassment, or just plain geography (since my parents were over 1000 miles away), but I didn't tell them how bad it had gotten and I didn't consider moving back home.

Just imagine what it felt like to be me back then. My only credit card was maxed out, my bank account was over drawn, and there was no cash in my wallet. I was living out of my truck, eating off of a case of Bush's baked beans. To open the can, I used one of those cheap can openers that hurts your fingers when you turned the knob. The blade seemed to always slide off the edge and it took several minutes just to open one aluminum can. The beans were cold because I didn't have any way to heat them up. I used a plastic spoon from Wendy's to dig out the beans. Those were some dark days. I would cry myself to sleep each night, wondering how I ever got myself into that mess.

A friend, who knew my situation, recommended I go to church. At first reluctant, I changed my tune when I considered that they may have free donuts or snacks for new guests. So with the few ounces of gas left in my truck's tank, I drove to Christ Church on Old Hickory Boulevard in Brentwood, TN. Not having frequented church as a kid, I didn't really know what to expect. At first I was very nervous about the experience because people were singing, raising their hands, and as I later learned, were in the "praise and worship" part of the service. I settled into the far back row of the second floor of the sanctuary, wondering when the donuts would arrive. The pastor got behind the pulpit and began to preach. It felt like he was speaking directly to me and my situation (even though there were more than 500 people in attendance at that Sunday morning service). By the end, he asked for anyone looking to make a change in their life to walk down to the front of the stage and give their heart to Christ. I was sold on what he was offering so I walked all the way down and gave my heart to Christ. At the time, I didn't know exactly what I was agreeing to, but I knew I needed help and I was desperate. I thought to myself, "Nothing else has been working out lately so maybe this will?"

With the hubbub of walking down that aisle, I forgot about the donuts, the original reason why I attended church, but, I did walk out of there a new man. With my new lease on life, I reassessed my situation and decided I needed some money coming in. I got a job as a valet because it paid immediate cash and a friend recommended I referee pee-wee football because that also paid instantaneously. Soon I was eating food other than cold beans. What's more, this experience of going homeless had taught me that I needed help if I was going to succeed in real estate. I discovered that pulling oneself up by his bootstraps was not what truly successful people did. Successful people don't go it alone, they reach out for help. I needed to truly educate myself with more than just books from the library. I needed the help of another person who had done what I wanted to do. I began searching for a mentor, someone who could take me by the hand and show me the ropes. Have you ever heard of the saying, "When the student is ready, the teacher arrives?"

Right about that time, I had located a property well under value. I had put it under contract to purchase for $30,000. The value of the property could be as much as $90,000 if it was all fixed up. I didn't have the time, money or expertise to renovate the house though. A local investor recommended I "flip" the property, or re-sell the property to another investor. This technique would provide me with quick cash and I wouldn't need the time, money or expertise required to fix up the property.

I put the word out and the details of this deal found its way to a gentleman who was randomly in Nashville because his mother was battling cancer. This guy had come from five generations of real estate investors. He was a Nashville native, but had been living on the beach in Florida for the past several years. He was a street smart person and knew how to make money.

In fact, he was so common sense intelligent that he made more than $180,000 on his first real estate deal when he was only 18 years old. He put a corner lot owned by Exxon under contract for $100,000 and then flipped the parcel to an adjacent property owner for $280,000. How many 18 year olds do that? This person knew business and he knew real estate.

As I was showing him the property I wanted him to buy, he began asking me questions about what I was doing. It didn't take long for me to spill the beans and share with him how bad things had gotten. He was shocked to find out I was a Vanderbilt graduate with a degree in mechanical engineering choosing to go homeless for my dream of becoming a real estate investor. He said, "If you have enough determination to stick with your goal of being a real estate investor to the point of going homeless, I can show you how to make real money in real estate." He went on to propose, "If you agree to split profits with me, we can do something together." And before he finished that sentence, he chimed in with, "Oh, and also don't do anything to get me sued. I don't need the hassle. I can live on the beach with my dog and my Bible, not work and be just fine, so don't do anything that would tie me into a lawsuit." I agreed to his terms.

My arrangement with him was such that he agreed to take me by the hand and show me step by step how to be a real estate investor. My job was to listen to him, however outrageous I thought his instructions were, and do all the legwork and then we would split the profits 50/50. I'll never forget what he told me that first day. He said, "50% of something is a whole lot more than a 100% of nothing." That lesson right there changed my life and it will also change your financial life too. As I later discovered, the principle he was sharing stretches to almost every type of business. The greatest fortunes were built by sharing the profits. Did you know that at the height of Standard Oil, John D Rockefeller was only a 1/6th owner in the company? Wealthy people don't try to own 100% of a small pie; they instead, align themselves with great people and together take a portion of a much larger pie. 50% of something is a whole lot more than a 100% of nothing.

Here was that principle in action. Our first deal together didn't at first appear to be a good deal at all. It was a very well built country house on sixteen acres in the rolling hills of Franklin, TN. The owner had built the property to be his family's dream home and for several years it was just that. But, his financial situation had changed and he began to struggle to make ends meet. He hired a real estate agent to sell the property and for more than one year, the property sat on the market at a list price of $300,000. The total mortgage balance on the property was about $275,000. The seller had two loans. The first mortgage was an interest only loan with a principal balance of $225,000 and the second mortgage was a home equity line of credit (also known as a HELOC) with a balance of $50,000. Together, his total monthly payment was about $1,500 and at the time, he was falling several months behind.

When the deal first crossed my path, it had come to me through another real estate investor in town. I had spread the word out among other investors in my area that if they had any potential deals they didn't want, to send them to me and if I could turn these discarded deals into money, they would get a referral fee when they closed. In other words, I was asking for their junk leads they were already throwing in the garbage. The concept did generate some leads for me, but most of them were of no value.

I mentioned this lead to my new mentor thinking it was worthless, but to my surprise, he said, "Go sign it up. I smell an opportunity." That was his way of saying, "Get the property under contract." One of the beautiful aspects of real estate is that you can control property without having to own it so long as you use the right paperwork. Furthermore, if your contracts have the appropriate clauses in them, you can make the process of getting a property under contract virtually risk-free. On his recommendation, I made the drive to the property, met with the sellers and offered to purchase their property for the amount they owed. I gave the sellers all the cash I had for earnest money, $1.

Rather than turning me down, I was pleasantly surprised to see the sellers agree. They were a bit suspicious since the property had been listed for over a year with a very well respected real estate agent and wasn't selling and here was a young kid ready to buy it after only viewing the property for a few minutes, but they needed to sell and were open to just about anything. I, however, was somewhat indifferent since I had experienced so many real estate failures up until that point that I wasn't going to get all that excited until the money was in my bank account. I was still impressed though that I could tie up a piece of property so easily.

"OK, what next?" I asked my mentor. He reviewed the details of the deal and determined we needed to see if the second mortgage would take less than their full payoff to release their lien from the property. This is now a much more common phrase in real estate, often referred to as a "short sale", but at the time, there wasn't a name for it. Back then, you simply contacted the department that handled the loans that were in default and you negotiated a reduced payoff (nowadays, it is far more organized and most lending institutions have entire departments that just handle short sale requests). Since the seller had not paid the second mortgage for several months, the loan was already assigned to the default department.

My mentor told me to offer 10% of $50,000, or $5,000. I took his advice but didn't think the bank would accept. Sure enough, they did! The mortgage company faxed a letter stating they would accept $5,000 for their $50,000 second mortgage. Jackpot! Or was it? Where was I going to come up with $5,000?

Rather than give me $5,000, my mentor wanted me to learn how to be self-sufficient, how to be a real estate investor, even though I didn't have money to invest or the ability to qualify for a real estate loan. He introduced me to the concept of offering a "rent to own." The key ingredient to this concept was locating a "tenant buyer," someone who wanted to be a homeowner but was struggling to qualify for a home loan. To round up some candidates, he instructed me to put out hand written signs on a Friday afternoon at busy street corners near the property that said "Rent to Own" as well as a phone number (this was before Craigslist and other online classifieds).

Then, another shocking result occurred. The phone rang off the hook, literally. I fielded incoming calls for several days. It had worked. Some simple, handwritten signs had generated an overwhelming response. After a few meetings with tenant buyers that went nowhere, my mentor told me I needed to concentrate on people who had a down payment above $10,000 since we had to payoff the second mortgage of $5,000 as well as catch up the back payments on the first mortgage which amounted to $4,800. He also said that although there would be far fewer of these people, they would be a better use of my time and I only needed one tenant buyer to do this deal. There's a great lesson in real estate. You only need one buyer to make a deal happen. You only need one.

After pouring through a large number of callers who didn't fit that description, I finally discovered someone who said they had $20,000 to put down. A bit skeptical, I set up a time to meet, but thought to myself, "Who, on earth, has $20,000 available in cash but can't buy a home the traditional way?" Since cell phone coverage was spotty out in the country where that property was situated, we met at a nearby McDonalds and they were to follow me to the actual property.

While on the drive, I prayed for a miracle. I was still struggling to survive, living day by day. The gas tank was so empty that I was almost certain I wouldn't be able to get back home. I was so broke there wasn't even any change in the glove box. I didn't know what I would do if I ran out of gas.

Trailing behind me was a slightly beat up Tahoe with a couple inside who had said they did contract work for Lowe's. They brought in what banks consider self employed income which made it very difficult for them to get a traditional mortgage. Banks far prefer the W2 income that is generated from having a normal job. We drove out past the developments and into the countryside that Tennessee is known for. There were large horse farms bordered by white wooden fences stretched as far as the eye could see. We moved deeper and deeper into the country as we headed toward the property.

I had shown this home before to a few other couples but they had all commented that the property was too far out in the country for them. So I thought its rural setting was a negative. The further we drove into the sticks, the more concerned I got that I would look in the rear view mirror and that Tahoe would be gone. But thankfully, they stayed in tow.

We arrived at the entrance to the driveway. On one side of the road was an old, half full, completely dilapidated garbage truck. The neighbor across the street ran a garbage business and this foul smelling landmark was one of their latest equipment failures. So if you had your window down, on your way in, you'd get a fresh whiff of trash. Since my AC was acting up, I definitely got a whiff.

The actual sixteen acres was not square in shape, but more of a long, rectangular parcel. The house was situated at the highest point of the plot of land, far back from the road. The dirt driveway hugged along the left edge of the property and wound slowly upward before ending at the left side of the home. My truck began to crawl down the long driveway with the crunching sound of tires rolling over gravel filing the air. The truck began to distance itself from the Tahoe behind me, not only because I had been there a few times already and felt more comfortable navigating the winding dirt road, but also because they were inspecting every detail of the property.

I had already parked and was looking back at their progress when something magical occurred. Three small deer pranced across the driveway, right in front of their vehicle. It was as if I had staged the experience, with a walkie-talkie in hand, telling an associate, "Queue the deer." But it wasn't planned. I had nothing to do with 3 deer running across the property. It was a miracle.

The husband and wife emerged from their vehicle with a gigantic smile on their face. They took in a deep breath, the way vacationers do when camping in the mountains. As it turns out, this was exactly what they were looking for in a home. They wanted to be out in the country with lots of land.

After briefly reviewing the inside of the home, they came back to me and said, "We'll take it. Who do we make the check out to?"

I was speechless. It worked! This actually worked! Right before my very eyes, this couple wrote out a $20,000 check to me personally. I said to myself, "What do I do now?" After catching my breath from all the excitement, I knew I needed some cash that day just to survive, so rather than deposit the check and wait several business days for the check to clear, I went to the bank the check was drawn on and cashed it. Have you ever had $20,000 cash in an envelope before? It's a unique experience. I was paranoid someone was following me and was going to nab that money. When I got to my bank, the teller, to which had seen my average account balance the past 12 months on her computer screen, looked with amazement (and suspicion) as I handed over $20,000 in cash for deposit. And just like that, there was real money in my bank account.

Since the property was vacant by this time, the rent to own tenant buyers moved in right away. $5,000 was sent to the second mortgage to pay off the loan and then $4,800 was sent to the first mortgage to catch up the back payments. The tenant buyers agreed to pay $1,800 per month and our total monthly payment which included the first mortgage payment, taxes and insurance, was $1,300 each month. So we profited about $10,200 immediately plus $500 per month. Meanwhile, I didn't have to qualify for a loan or use any of my own cash to purchase the property. I was becoming a real estate investor!

We referred the tenant buyers to a mortgage broker to help them get on the path to being able to get a loan to payoff the rest of the property. In 3 months, the mortgage broker had qualified them for a loan. She had found a special loan program for self employed people. The tenant buyers had agreed to pay $275,000 for the property and since they had already put down $20,000, they only needed a loan for $255,000. The first mortgage balance we had to pay off was $225,000. After closing costs, we were looking at earning about $25,000 when the tenant buyers' loan went through.

Right before the closing, there was another twist. The title company had noticed a very odd detail in the recorded loan paperwork. The legal description on the paperwork described the neighbor's property. In other words, the first mortgage was on the little neighbor's home, not the sixteen acres and beautiful country home. I was not sure how this was going to help anything but my mentor had a plan. He reasoned that we could potentially negotiate a lower payoff since the attorneys fees the bank would incur to correct the paperwork could run into the tens of thousands. With a few phone calls, sure enough, the first mortgage reduced their payoff to $206,000. This last minute first mortgage payoff reduction put another $19,000 profit in our pockets.

In all, this deal netted more than $56,000. I didn't borrow any money, didn't qualify for a loan, didn't use any cash to acquire the property and everyone was happy with the outcome. The sellers were happy to have sold the property without owing anything, the new buyers purchased their dream home and we had made a ton of money!

Had it not been for my mentor, I would have received 100% of nothing. Instead, I was $28,000 richer, an amount some people work an entire year at their job to earn. That was the largest amount of money I had ever put into my bank account up to that point in my life. I would go to the ATM just to check my balance because I couldn't believe my eyes.

Interestingly enough, about a year later, I followed back up with those rent to own tenant buyers who had purchased the property and innocently asked how they were getting along with all those deer running across their property. She replied, "Since that day you showed us this property for the first time, we've only seen deer here one other time." Do you believe in miracles?

Think of all the different parts of my first deal with my mentor that most people would never have imagined would have worked. First, that a seller would so easily have sold their home to me with $1 earnest money. Second, that the second mortgage would have accepted $5,000 for a $50,000 loan. Third, that I could sell a property in a few weeks that a top notch real estate agent couldn't after over a year. Fourth, that there would be people out there who can't qualify for a traditional mortgage but have money to put down and can afford the monthly payment. Fifth, that a first mortgage would reduce their payoff due to incorrect loan paperwork. That's one of the powerful aspects of having a mentor. They teach you things you didn't know you didn't know. It turns out that all of those details can be fairly common in real estate under the right circumstances. While most people may never imagine that such series of events could ever come together, for experienced real estate investors, they are considered everyday occurrences.

After that first deal together, we were off to the races. He guided and mentored me to more money than I could have ever dreamed. We did all types of deals: short sales, foreclosures, wholesales, rehabs, lease purchases and creative finance deals. You name it, we did it all. Life was good. With my new found freedom, I traveled, enjoyed life and then met the woman of my dreams and got married.

One day, my wife and I asked ourselves, "Since we can, if there is any place in the world we could live, where would we live and why?" Have you ever asked yourself that question? It's not as easy of an answer as you may think. After several years of deliberation, we decided on a beachfront community in Florida where we bought a mansion on the water (it was a distressed property that we got for about half of its value, of course). It's paradise for us and I surf and fish as much as my wife will allow. *Side note gentlemen: Happy wife = Happy life.*

Each time I would be in an airplane, I would see thousands of homes scattered in all directions. On one particular flight, this thought popped into my mind, "How can I do deals all across the country?" I could see that there were thousands of cities and thousands of homes in each one of those cities. How could I be a part of making money on all those deals?

My first approach was to build a company with employees. Since I could do deals long distance, without ever seeing the property myself in person, my plan was to train my employees on what to do. I began hiring people. Soon, I noticed that my plan was not working out well. What I learned was that employees did about 75% of what I would do, despite how well I trained them. In real estate, 75% doesn't cut it. For a deal to close, someone had to be on top of the details and I found that 9 to 5 employees didn't have any major incentive to take care of the little details to ensure deals closed. They were paid to show up, not to perform.

Then, I had an "ah-ha" moment. I reasoned that perhaps the best way to expand across the country would not be to hire employees, but instead, to mentor those interested in becoming real estate investors the way my mentor did for me. We could split the profits 50/50 and now, instead of a 75% employee that did just enough to not get fired, I would have a business partner that was 100% committed to the financial success of each deal. Plus, I would be passing on a set of skills that could benefit the people I mentored. Not only could I gain economically from this new approach, but also I could pass on a legacy of having helped others achieve their dreams. In hindsight, it seems like such an obvious solution, but at the time, it was a revolutionary idea for me.

As always, great ideas include great challenges. Being a successful real estate investor is much different from being a great real estate mentor. It's one thing to be able to do something yourself. It's a completely different challenge to be able to teach someone else how to do it. There were many years of trial and error as I crafted a system for teaching others how to be a real estate investor. Not only did each task, technique, and strategy have to be simplified, it also had to work most, if not all of the time. Anytime you teach someone else a subject, you have to know it so much more thoroughly. It was like being mentored all over again; only this time, my mentors were the students I was teaching.

Mentoring someone outside of your own backyard, in a completely different area with different laws, demographics and market dynamics was another huge challenge for me too. There were many mistakes made, but I grew from them. And, eventually, I made some breakthroughs. Although, the majority of real estate investing is universal, each area is also unique. Some strategies work better in some areas, but not as well in others. In the beginning, I looked at this as a handicap, but now, it has become a strength. I mentor from a nationwide perspective so I see more opportunities oftentimes than those that only see the narrow, local view. You also have more resources at a nationwide level, such as closing companies, mortgage brokers and many other critical team members that allow us to complete creative transactions that oftentimes a local closing company or mortgage broker is unable to do. Sometimes in life, what you think is going to be a hindrance to your success becomes one of the reasons for your success.

I so appreciate all those students in the beginning who endured the kinks and glitches first hand. Thankfully, despite those initial growing pains, my students experienced extraordinary results. And, as luck would have it, teaching others comes naturally to me. At least that is what my students have told me.

In addition to the success of my early students, a few rose above the crowd and truly impressed me with their own creativity and ingenuity. They had taken what they had learned from me and then added their own entrepreneurial touch to it. I was always told to surround myself with great people and so for those students that truly shined and had a heart for teaching, I invited them to coach with me. Together, spread out across the country (but connected by phone and internet), we efficiently and effectively mentor and coach budding real estate investors to success.

Today, we operate one of the most innovative and results producing real estate education companies ever created. We offer stand alone training courses as well as coaching and mentoring programs where we split profits with our students. Each year, people from all walks of life experience true financial breakthroughs as a result of our educational programs. They become independent, highly successful real estate investors, living their dreams. What an honor and privilege it is to be a part of transforming people's financial lives.

Now you know where the author is coming from when you read this book. Not only have I personally experienced a rags-to-riches journey with real estate, I have also proven that it wasn't a fluke by teaching others to be successful real estate investors as well. Amidst thousands of deals and thousands of students through up and down markets, this book comes from the real world of real estate investing. It's the book I wish was available and I would have read when I first got started. It's a book that tells the real story of how to successfully invest in real estate.

Although I haven't read EVERY published real estate investing book, I can safely say that most of the ones I have read don't tell the whole story. For some, I don't blame the author. He or she simply didn't have the distinct opportunity to be as fully immersed in as many different types of deals, with as many people in as many different areas over such a long period of time as I have. For others, like the ones I read when I was first getting started, they focused entirely on the positive aspects of investing but failed to communicate the challenges as well. The goal of this book is to tell the whole story, the good and the bad.

You'll find that success in real estate is not dependant on the area you live in, or the current market conditions, or your cash position, or your credit score, or the way you talk, or how charismatic you are, or anything like that. Instead, you'll discover that becoming a successful real estate investor involves thinking like and doing what other successful investors do. Real estate is rarely a get-rich-quick endeavor, but when you stick with it, it is usually a stay rich long term experience. Apply what you learn in this book and you'll have a set of skills you can take with you the rest of your life that can help you live the life of your dreams. Welcome to the wonderful world of real estate investing!

Part 1: Why Be a Real Estate Investor?

"90% of all millionaires become so through owning real estate."
– Andrew Carnegie

Why should you become a real estate investor? There are, after all, many different ways to make more money in life. Statistics released by the foremost authority on personal finance, the Internal Revenue Service, revealed that the majority of personal wealth of US taxpayers is held in real estate. Has the thought of running your own business, being your own boss, or calling your own shots ever crossed your mind? The IRS further points out that the most likely way for anyone to become independently wealthy in one lifetime is through entrepreneurship and through owning your own business. Opportunity seekers can spend countless hours researching the best paths for making money. If you are one of those people, you can stop your research. Becoming a real estate entrepreneur provides you with the highest probability for economic prosperity.

One of the reasons why real estate is so good for making money is that it is the IDEAL investment.

Income: Real estate can provide you with steady, tax advantaged income, often referred to as *cash flow*. You can rent real estate to a tenant. Overtime, rental payments from that tenant can payoff your mortgage, cover any property management and maintenance costs, and can still leave enough for you to have a steady income as well. Although there are other investments that provide steady income, such as bonds, and stocks that offer dividends, real estate typically provides a larger amount of income than bond coupon payment or stock dividends and is more tax advantaged.

Depreciation: This term is used for tax purposes and is of great value to real estate investors. To illustrate the concept of depreciation, think of the life span of a t-shirt. After being worn and washed, over the course of several years, it deteriorates. Although you may have t-shirts that have lasted decades, the average t-shirt probably lasts a couple of years. For determining how much you will pay in taxes on your real estate investment, the IRS has recognized that the structure of a property (not the land, just the structure) deteriorates too, and they set the life span of a residential rental property at 27 ½ years. Does a well maintained house simply crumble to the ground after 27 ½ years? Of course not. But for determining how much you will be paying the IRS, whatever you bought the property for (minus the land), can be depreciated over 27 ½ years.

Example: You buy a $100,000 single family home and the land is worth $10,000. That means, for tax purposes, your tax basis (what you bought the structure for) is $90,000. When you divide $90,000 by 27 ½ years, you get a tax deduction of $3,272.73 per year for depreciation. If that same single family home has a positive cash flow of $270 per month, or $3,000 per year, you get to add an additional expense to that property in the form of depreciation for $3,240 and therefore, in this example, you don't have to pay any income taxes on the $270 per month you were bringing in! This is how real estate rental income is so incredibly tax advantageous.

With all the tax increases and unfair taxing rules, why would the government continue to allow this deduction for real estate investors? The government is giving people an incentive to be real estate owners. They want you to be a real estate investor.

Equity: When you buy real estate, you have the opportunity to purchase property at a price lower than its market value. When you get a good deal, the difference between what you bought it for and what it is worth is called equity. The old saying, "In real estate, you make your money when you buy," applies here. When you buy a property well below market value, you instantly get equity.

By comparison, publically traded stocks are purchased at market value. The market may be undervaluing or overvaluing the stock at the time of purchase, but either way, at the exact moment a stock is purchased, the price paid is what the market will pay for it. With real estate, however, you can buy a property well below market value and literally turn around and resell that same property for tens of thousands of dollars more a few moments later. We do this quite often, actually.

Appreciation: Over the course of the last hundred years, studies have shown that overall, residential real estate has kept pace with inflation. In some areas, residential property values have even appreciated above and beyond inflation. For wise and educated investors, appreciation is an added financial bonus to being a real estate owner, not the reason to buy property. Since predicting the future has proved to be a difficult task, buying real estate based on the other factors outlined earlier is a far better decision then betting on if or when a property will appreciate. You can only benefit from real estate appreciation if you own it. Therefore, owning as much real estate as you can, as wisely as you can, can give you the best probability of gaining from appreciation. And if it comes your way, be appreciative.

Leverage: When you borrow money to buy real estate, you are using leverage. The people and companies of this world that control the majority of the money, such as banks, mortgage companies, hedge funds, mutual funds, pension funds, insurance companies and private individuals, want to lend you money to buy real estate. That's how many of them make their money; by lending money to you on real estate. There are all different types of real estate lenders, from those that require good credit, lots of money and a great loan application all the way to those who simply lend money on real estate based on the market value of the property. If, for example, you buy a $100,000 property and you put down $10,000, you are using leverage to own a $100,000 asset with only $10,000 of your own money. The ability to borrow money to buy real estate is the use of leverage and it allows you to buy more real estate with less money.

Real estate truly is the IDEAL investment. That is just one of the many reasons why real estate is so attractive. Here are several other reasons why real estate investing may be exactly what you have been looking for in a business opportunity or investment vehicle.

Real estate investing doesn't discriminate based on your age, background or ethnicity. You're not too old or too young (although you must be 18 years old to own property.) Regardless of where you come from, how old you are, or what nationality you are, you're on a level playing field with everyone else.

Real estate investing requires no resume. It doesn't matter where you went to school, how many jobs you have had, the lack of professional skills you may have, or the color and texture of your resume paper. Successful investors come from all walks of life. You're not inferior if you lack higher levels of education. My mentor never went to college. If you have a college or post college degree, that's not a handicap either. Everyone is on a level playing field, regardless of what you're resume looks like.

Buying and selling real estate does not always involve the use of your cash or credit. There are several strategies that you will learn in this book that allow you to not only make fast money but also own real estate for long term wealth accumulation without having to put down any cash or borrow any money. Certainly, when an investor has cash and/or good credit, they will have more ways to invest in real estate, but as you learned from my personal story, it is possible for you to get started from absolute economic ground zero.

Real estate is a basic human necessity. As the saying goes, "Everyone needs a roof over their head." This book will focus on residential real estate investing. Living quarters come in all shapes and sizes too, from single family homes, to duplexes, condos, townhomes, apartments, co-ops, and much more. Real estate, unlike many other businesses and investments, provides something that absolutely everyone needs, shelter.

Real estate is everywhere, including where you live. A common misconception beginners have is, "Real estate investing doesn't work in my area." Non-sense! There is opportunity right under your nose. There are diamonds in your own backyard. In fact, once you learn and apply the techniques and strategies described in this book, you will be shocked at how much money you can make with real estate right within your own community. Believe it or not, you have been driving past real estate opportunities everyday. Real estate opportunities are everywhere, including where you live.

You can invest in real estate close to home or far away. You are not confined to just your area. Although we recommend beginners start in an area they are very familiar with, you have the ability to buy and sell real estate anywhere.

Disclaimer: This book will focus on techniques that work in the United States and Canada. I'm not familiar with investing in countries other than those two.

You can make money in up and down markets. When the real estate market is up, certain strategies work very well and then in down markets, other techniques become more productive. Regardless of the market, you can be successful investing in real estate.

Becoming a real estate investor does not require much in the way of equipment to get started. If you have a computer, a printer and a phone, you have all the equipment you need to begin. You can work from home, a coffee shop, or even your truck! Compare this to starting most any other business, which usually requires commercial space, a lease, staff, inventory, equipment, etc.

Launching a real estate investing operation is far simpler than starting the majority of businesses that have the potential to create comparable financial rewards. It doesn't require venture capital, a board of directors or even a detailed business plan. In fact, your investing plan could be sketched out on a napkin.

Investing in real estate doesn't have to be a full time activity. You can invest on the side, in your spare time. Overtime, you may come to enjoy it so much that you want to do it full time, but it's not necessary. In other words, you don't have to quit your day job to give real estate investing a try. You can invest with the limited spare time you have available.

And perhaps most important to most people, real estate can make you very rich and/or provide the lifestyle you have always wanted. Reviewing the list of the world's richest people, many on the list created their wealth in real estate. Many of the people with the biggest houses in your area made their money or maintain their wealth from real estate. Also, many of the people you meet on the street that are financially free come from a real estate background.

You may be asking, "So if real estate is so good, how come everyone isn't doing it?" That is a very good question. Real estate has some barriers-to-entry (a fancy business term to describe what makes a business difficult for competitors to break into).

Real estate investing, like any business, requires very specific knowledge. This knowledge is rarely taught in school. Most people simply do not know how to be a real estate investor. And, the education process requires both study and application. Much like chemistry in high school, where you had the lecture and then the laboratory, gaining the specific knowledge of real estate investing requires both absorbing educational materials as well as applying what you learn and experiencing it in the real world. Some concepts and ideas can rarely be acquired simply by reading about it. You have to get out there and experience it.

Investing in real estate requires patience. We live in a world obsessed with instant gratification. Real estate is not instant gratification. Usually the efforts you put forth several months ago reward you today. Some half-committed would-be investors give up when they are just a few days from collecting a huge payday. I have seen this phenomenon over and over again. Some people simply do not have the patience to see their real estate investing efforts turn into extraordinary financial returns.

Becoming a real estate investor means that you are starting your own business. And like any business owner will tell you, financial rewards from a business come from results. This is quite different from the way most people are compensated in life, which is based on activity; either an hourly or salary wage. Business owners are paid based on the results their business provides in the marketplace. Successful business owners think differently from wage earners.

For most people, the biggest hurdle in starting their own enterprise is not the physical aspect of completing the tasks, but the mental work of re-wiring their brains to think like a productive business owner. As Henry Ford said, "Thinking is the hardest work there is, which is why so few people do it." Understanding how to think like an investor is so important, I have devoted the entire next chapter to it.

Real estate is truly the most powerful vehicle that anyone can use to produce financial prosperity. In order to take advantage of the many opportunities real estate presents you must have the right education and your mind must be wired for productive real estate business ownership. The remainder of this book will be devoted to providing an extension of knowledge regarding those two aspects of real estate: having an investing mindset and educating yourself in the specific areas that will lead you to prosperity.

Part 2: How to Think Like an Investor

"Man's greatness lies in his power of thought." - Blaise Pascal

In my early years of teaching real estate to budding entrepreneurs, I would skip over the mental aspect of investing and get right into the meat of real estate. It was a mistake. What I discovered was that mentoring people on the mechanics of real estate investing was fairly straight forward. Once they had the instructions on what to do, the difference between those who succeeded and failed was largely due to what was going on inside their head.

Having all the knowledge on how to invest will be worthless unless you have your head straight. Before you can be a real estate investor, you have to think like one. That little space between your ears is extremely powerful and unfortunately, it doesn't come with an instruction manual. The following chapter is your instruction manual on how to operate your brain so that you can be a successful real estate entrepreneur. Plus, at the end of this chapter, you will have an opportunity to test your mental skills with an Investor IQ exam.

Your *Why*

Why should come before *what*. Why you want to do something is far more important than what you are going to do. We humans tend to get excited about new endeavors and then after the new-ness wears off, we tend to move onto something else. Most great achievements in life do not happen overnight. In fact, it's usually the exact opposite.

Your greatest triumphs probably took time to come together, right? Real estate investing is no different. After the excitement dulls and new-ness of real estate fades, what is going to be the reason, or reasons, for you to continue pursuing your goal of being a successful real estate investor?

When I first got started, I wanted to work from anywhere, have control over my time, be my own boss, call my own shots, earn what I was worth, make a whole lot of money and become financially free. That's not to much to ask, is it? At my j-o-b, I had to show up at the office, I couldn't work from anywhere. I had no control over my time. I didn't call my own shots. The boss told me what to do. I wasn't able to earn what I was worth, make a whole lot of money or become financially free. I earned what my salary was and the only way to improve that was to hope for a raise. These were strong reasons for me when I began. I didn't want to go back to that life again and this drove me to do what it took to succeed.

Why do you want to be a real estate investor? Are you in a similar situation as I was when I first got started? Or are you happy with your job and simply want to invest your hard earned money into an investment that produces better returns than you are currently getting? Are you concerned that your current financial plan will not create enough money for retirement? Do you want more time with loved ones? More money? More freedom to travel, explore and enjoy life? Your reason for becoming a real estate investor is your *Why*.

In order for your *Why* to be effective, it must be emotional. Emotions drive our behavior. When you harness this power, you can achieve extraordinary feats, well beyond what you may think is possible. Rather than relying on others to motivate you, the beauty of finding your *Why* is that any motivation you would ever want is already inside of you. You simply need to discover what your *Why* is to gain access to this unlimited resource of power.

You're looking for what you really want for your life that you don't already have. It can be positive or negative. Maybe you want to live everyday in a tropical paradise, lounging in a hammock between two palms trees, staying cool from a gentle island breeze. That may create significant positive emotions in you and the thought of creating that life for yourself may be the needed drive behind your success. But, perhaps, what's more important to you right now is getting out of debt and paying for your children's college. The pain you may feel for not being debt free and not currently having the financial resources to pay for your child's college education may be weighing on your heavily. These negative emotions can drive you to succeed as well.

In fact, psychologists tell us that negative emotions are stronger motivators than positive ones. Believe it or not, most people will be more driven to leave their job than to strive for a goal of financial freedom. You can use this knowledge to your advantage by first thinking about all the parts of your life that you don't like that you feel becoming a real estate investor could solve. A negative and very emotional *Why* can be all the motivation you'll ever need to succeed in real estate.

Take a moment to write down your *Why*. The more emotional you get about this *Why*, the better your outcome will be. This needs to burn inside of you every time you think of it. It could be as simple as how frustrated you are with the way your retirement fund investments have been performing and just the thought of lackluster results gets you boiling mad. Or, it could be as significant as not being able to be with your loved ones nearly as often as you want to because of your current financial condition. If nothing is coming to mind right now, spend some time each day for the next few weeks thinking about it until you find it.

Without a *Why*, chances are, you won't take the actions necessary to becoming a successful real estate investor. It's that important. When someone is completely comfortable, they rarely have strong enough reasons to do anything different than what they are already doing. Finding your hot buttons, what really makes you uncomfortable about your current situation, is the fastest and easiest way to have and maintain consistent motivation. You need to find your *Why*. Make this your first priority for becoming a real estate investor.

Pain and Pleasure

The two basic motivating forces in our lives are pain and pleasure. We choose to do something either because of the pleasure we think we are going to gain from the action or the pain we believe we are going to avoid by taking that action. For example, your *Why* may be something along the lines of wanting to fulfill the dream of living everyday on the beach with the sun and the sand. That is an example of striving to gain pleasure. On the other hand, your *Why* could be that you never want to be poor and have to barely get by in life again. That is an example of wanting to avoid pain. As simple as this concept may sound, this is precisely how our brains work.

Applying this simple but extremely powerful concept can open up an entirely new world for you. You can learn to motivate yourself in ways you never thought possible. For example, most new investors struggle with the paralyzing affects of fear. They fear talking to a motivated seller, getting a contract signed, asking for non-refundable earnest money from a buyer, etc. The problem is that so much advice centers around *thinking positive*. Simply *thinking positive* can sometimes push you to ignore reality in an attempt to eliminate fear. There is no need to blind ourselves to the realities of life. On the contrary, fear can be very useful to us. Fear can be a great counselor and guide.

Rather than eliminate fear, why not use it as a motivator? Instead of worrying, "What do I say to this homeowner?," use fear as your motivation and think, "If I don't call this person, it could cost me $30,000 and that would absolutely devastate me and plus, I need the money." Avoiding pain is a much stronger motivator than striving to gain pleasure. Most people will fight much harder to get back $20,000 that someone stole from them than to save little by little until they have built up $20,000 in their bank account. You are far more driven to avoid pain than to gain pleasure. Use this knowledge to motivate yourself to take action.

Specifically, when you hit a juncture in your investing journey whereby fear begins to slow you down or even paralyze you, immediately begin to think of all the things you will lose by not taking the action. Really think deeply about it until you start to feel the pain that will occur if you don't take the action. For example, for some beginners (and some seasoned investors, sadly), asking for non-refundable earnest money from buyers is very nerve racking and scary, even though it shouldn't be. (Ironically, once an investor is burned once by a buyer who walks away from a deal and leaves the investor high and dry, never again is that investor concerned about demanding non-refundable earnest money.)

Here's how to utilize the power of avoiding pain to drive a new investor to get non-refundable earnest money from a prospective buyer. They can have the following conversation in their head, "If I don't demand non-refundable earnest money from this buyer, I will potentially allow this buyer to back out of the deal scot-free and that will cost me $37,000 as well as the time I have spent getting this deal to where it is at and not to mention hurting the homeowner who is counting on me to help him." Do you see how you can use fear and pain as drivers to help you take action? Rather than ignoring pain and fear, take control of it and it will change your life.

Your Comfort Zone

Have you ever known someone that *knew* what to do but simply wasn't doing it? Has that person ever been you, maybe, at times? If so, why did you fall into the trap of inactivity when you absolutely knew what you were supposed to do? The answer is somewhere deep down in your mind. You linked up or associated pain to that action step so that even though you knew how to do the task, you didn't do it because your brain didn't want you to. Our brains are always linking positive and negative emotions to our thoughts. Your mind is constantly attaching labels of "pleasure" or "pain" to each action you take.

For example, many new real estate investors have a fear of talking to property sellers. Instead of getting on the phone with the owner right away to get an understanding of the person's situation, many new investors will take part in the following scenario:

Get in their car, drive over to the house, check out the outside of the home, drive around and study the neighborhood, head back home and finally, do all sorts of research online about the property all before ever having spoken to the property owner.

This eats up hours of time, tons of energy as well as travel expenses and the crazy part is that the property owner may not even want to sell their property or maybe completely unrealistic in their demands! Why would anyone in their right mind spend all that time, energy and expense before picking up a phone and making one simple phone call and asking a few simple questions? This person obviously associates more pain to making that one simple phone call than the pain of all the time, energy, and expense they exerted. People will do far more to avoid pain than to gain pleasure.

To take the above example one step further, the one action that was most out-of-this-person's comfort zone was talking on the phone to the property owner. Driving around and researching online were both well within his/her comfort level. ***Your money zone will always equal your comfort zone.*** To continue to be successful in life, you'll have to be continually stepping out of your comfort zone. Your money zone will always equal your comfort zone.

Everyone has a different comfort zone. What if this person was unable to drive a vehicle? Then, the phone call would be far more comfortable than driving. What if this person had trouble navigating the Internet? Then, the phone call would have been far easier than researching online.

Hopefully your comfort zone encompasses all of the actions in this book. If not, resolve in your mind to be willing to step outside your comfort zone. That may involve getting better at communicating over the phone. That may include using the computer to organize your business online as opposed to just in paper files. The list could go on and on. You need to be willing to stretch yourself. Be open to the concept of stepping outside of your comfort zone. Why? There's that *Why* again. If you have already discovered your *Why*, you should have had an answer to why stepping outside of your comfort zone is so important. Moving from actions that are outside of your comfort zone to more actions outside your comfort zone is where you'll experience your greatest breakthroughs.

Attitude

Extremely successful real estate investors have a unique attitude on life. They view every experience as a test and then every result as a learning lesson. This attitude creates a mindset that does not recognize failure. It never produces phrases like, "Well, that was a waste." Nothing is a waste to an investor with the right attitude. Every experience is a test and every result is a lesson.

This attitude doesn't always create a positive, pleasurable feeling though. In fact, sometimes the lessons successful investors learn are painful, and rather than ignore the pain, they experience it so that they don't have to learn the lesson again. If a test produces a result you didn't expect, don't immediately assume it was bad. It could be frustrating and not enjoyable at the time, but later, you may look back and realize that the lesson you learned was so incredibly valuable and necessary for you to close the next deal that came along.

Successful investors have an attitude of gratitude as well. They are thankful to have the opportunity to invest. They are appreciative of the lessons they learn and the experiences they gain. When problems arise, they consider them as challenges and rather than complain, view such situations as opportunities to learn.

Action Over Analysis

The main reason why so many people don't take action is fear. It's the fear of the unknown, fear of making a mistake, and fear of moving outside of their comfort zone. Instead, what they should fear most is not taking action at all! Keep in mind that everyone has made mistakes when first embarking on a new journey. The more mistakes you make, the faster you learn. Your biggest fear then should become inaction. In fact, do you know what most successful investors' only real estate regret is? They wish they would have gotten started sooner.

A very common behavior amongst new investors is analysis paralysis. Rather than take action, the person analyzes, analyzes and then analyzes some more, to the point where they become paralyzed. It stems from the fear of making a mistake. These people also tend to read book after book and attend seminar after seminar but never actually buy a property or do a deal. They tell themselves that they are waiting until they know enough to be confident in order to start actually investing. In actuality, what these prospective investors fail to recognize is that they will never reach the level of knowing enough about real estate to be truly confident until they take action. The confidence that is gained from truly knowing what you are doing won't come from a book. It will come from taking action.

Continually educating yourself is vital to your long term success in real estate, but only if you are taking action while you are educating yourself. Investors are always learning new techniques, new distinctions, and new ways of investing. They never reach a point of complete understanding in all aspects of real estate. Therefore, waiting to take action until the point of complete confidence in knowing what to do will keep a person paralyzed indefinitely. Interestingly enough, we have discovered that investors with less knowledge but far less fear in trying new things and taking action actually produce far better and faster results than those investors with much more knowledge but less action. Action is far more powerful than analysis.

Commitment

Sam Walton, the founder of Wal-Mart, the largest retailer in the world, was quoted as saying, "Like every overnight success, it's usually 20 years in the making." His point was that success is a long term commitment. The greatest real estate investors the world has ever seen have all had one characteristic in common; they stuck with it until they succeeded. Simple, isn't it?

In order to ensure you reach your goals, you must be willing to make a sincere and binding commitment to stick with it until you are success. By contrast, what you should not say to yourself would sound something this, "I'll give this 3 months. If it works, then I'll keep doing it. If not, I'll go do something else." That is the opposite of a commitment and it's a surefire way to fail in any endeavor in life. Instead, if you really want to succeed, you must make a commitment that you will stick with real estate for as long as it takes *until* you are successful. The key word in that sentence is, "until." That's a commitment.

You want to be a finisher in a world of starters. Once you achieve success in this endeavor, once you finish, then choose to re-evaluate. That is how successful people think. They say to themselves, "I'll do this for as long as it takes until I am a success, then I can re-evaluate."

If you are serious about becoming a real estate investor, right here, right now, make a commitment to stick to this until you are successful. If you can make such a commitment to yourself, your family and your future, then you are on the road to greatness. Congratulations!

You can begin putting this new commitment into practice by finishing the reading of this book!

Possibility Thinking

Successful investors know that there are typically several reasons why a deal won't work and the real big money is made when they are able to discover at least one reason why the deal will work. I call this Possibility Thinking. It's the habit of asking yourself, "How can it work?" rather than dwelling on why something won't work. Unlike simply thinking positive, which can ignore reality and actually prevent growth, possibility thinking involves assessing the cold, hard facts of a situation and then coming up with creative ways to solve the problem. Here's a quick way to begin building your possibility thinking muscle. The next time you are negotiating or making a decision with another person, avoid using the word "no," and instead, replace with, "yes, but." This will force you to begin thinking creatively so that you can come up with more ways to solve problems. To be a successful real estate investor, you need to think in terms of possibilities.

An analogy to illustrate this point involves an experience I had while my wife was swimming with dolphins in the Florida Keys. The dolphins lived in a lagoon that connected directly to the ocean so that the dolphins were provided a completely natural habitat. The only barrier to the open ocean for these dolphins was a chain-linked fence that rose about 4 feet above the water. These dolphins, as part of their routine, performed choreographed jumps of up to 12 feet out of the water. I asked one of the trainers why the dolphins didn't just jump over the chain-linked fence into oceanic freedom? His response was, "I guess they have never been taught that trick." With real estate, any temporary roadblocks you may face will be much like the dolphin fence. They can be overcome because you have the ability to overcome them. Don't make the tragic mistake of allowing a simple four foot fence stop you from freedom.

Repetition

Repetition is the mother of skill. In order to get good at anything, you have to do it over and over again. Regardless of how well you think you learn, or how quick you feel like you retain new information, the key to mastery is repetition.

You'll find that reading the same information more than once can be remarkably enlightening. Plus, as your perspective changes, you will recognize concepts and ideas that never occurred to you before.

As you repeat the skills and techniques you learn from this book over and over again, eventually, they will get buried into your sub-conscious mind and then, you will be able to apply them on autopilot without even having to think about them. That's when real estate investing becomes easy, when you can basically do it in your sleep. The most successful investors have programmed their mind to think like an investor on autopilot. That comes with repetition.

Humility

Humility is an important part of an investor's mental toolkit. Throughout history, the list of famous people who have had great falls due to pride and arrogance are many. Being humble involves doing more listening than talking and being perceptive. It requires removing one's ego and avoiding making assumptions. Humility avoids being easily angered or troubled. It means that you embrace change, you welcome challenges, and you recognize that everything will not work out as you had planned.

Humility also allows you to learn from your mistakes and to open your mind to new ideas. It can be very difficult for someone who thinks they already know everything to allow new ideas into their minds. Some have referred to this behavior as having a cup that is full. You want to your cup to be empty. You want to allow new ideas in. Those with full cups fail miserably in real estate. Those with an empty cups give themselves the opportunity to learn new ideas and ultimately, to succeed.

Humility means that you don't blame others for your shortcomings in business. Instead, you blame yourself. This is how you grow as a successful investor; by taking responsibility for your successes (or failures) and having the character to grow from it.

Humility is not weakness. In fact, humility is a sign of strength. You can be humble and yet still be a poised, confident and assertive leader. However, there is a fine line between confidence and arrogance, between being sure of oneself and being full of oneself. Successful investors are confident and humble.

Taking Advice

Advice is a peculiar thing. Almost everyone has an opinion. But who is right? The simple answer is that the person who has already produced extraordinary results in a given field is usually the person most accurate in their opinions on that subject. For beginner real estate investors, the first few months are a very critical and fragile time in their development. It is here that many well intentioned friends, family members and associates will see the beginner embarking on this new journey and may express their opinions. If the beginner listens to the negative voices in their life, they may quit or at least pull back from giving it their full effort. The simplest way to avoid this devastating outcome is to always ask yourself if the person providing the advice is a reliable source on the subject. Has the person who is providing the opinion on real estate made an absolute fortune investing in real estate? If so, listen to that person. If not, don't. Ask yourself if the person providing the advice is a reflection of someone you want to be.

Ironically, sometimes the people most willing to advise new investors on the business of real estate are those who have failed miserably at it. Such as a local real estate agent who is barely making ends meet, or a friend who invested in a course and never used it or even a family member that heard of someone who had tried real estate and supposedly *real estate* didn't work. The only people you should ever take advice from on a subject are those people who have mastered that subject and are very successful with it.

For example, parents can be a great resource for advice on raising children but if your parents struggled financially their entire lives, they may not give the best advice on becoming financially free. Oftentimes, well-intentioned authority figures, such as parents, provide career and financial advice when they are not the most qualified to provide the assistance. Since we are raised to follow our parents' direction, it is natural to take money advice from parents. But are they qualified to provide advice on financial freedom? You may have a close friend that you confide in with life's biggest challenges. That person may be a wonderful shoulder to cry on, but are they fit to give you solid advice on becoming a successful investor? Beware of financial advice from broke people. It isn't rude or disrespectful to avoid heeding the advice of those who are not qualified to give the advice. Instead, it's responsible.

Therefore, as you begin this journey, make sure you verify the credentials of whoever is trying to advise you on real estate investing. If that person is not a master in the field in which they are speaking, do not act on their advice. They may, in fact, lead you astray. On the other hand, if a local attorney in your area who has successfully worked with real estate investors for the past half century advises you on your local market, this person may be a good source to get advice.

Once you have verified that the advice giver is a credible source, you now need to assess their reason for giving you the advice. Understanding where the advice giver is coming from is also an extremely important skill. Let's take the local real estate attorney example. What if, at the time you were seeking out the advice, that attorney was concerned about a new law that may be passed which would drastically alter the way he could advise his clients. He may be very cautious in his advice and not provide you all the details because of his underlying uncertainty. Or what about the unscrupulous real estate agent who wants to buy the property you located and tries to persuade you that the deal you found is not a good one but meanwhile, is planning to try to buy it as soon as you walk away.

It's like asking the barber if you need a haircut. Regardless of whether you need a haircut or not, you are asking a barber, who gets paid to cut people's hair. When you ask a barber if you need a haircut, his answer will usually be, "Precisely."

How do you combat bad advice from very well qualified advice givers? Align their interests with yours. If your local attorney stands to make money from you on deal after deal by closing your real estate transactions, he/she has a vested interest in giving you advice that will encourage you to do more deals. If the local real estate agent you are working with gets compensated for helping you buy the property or in helping re-sell the property once you buy it, you are aligning both of your interests. Successful real estate investors align the interests of all parties involved in a deal because they know that in the real world, most people do what's best for themselves. When the parties to a deal operate in their own best interest, it also helps everyone else because everyone's interests are aligned.

That's how we built our apprentice program, on mutually aligned interests. My students split their profits with us 50/50. When they win, we win. This ensures that my team and I give the absolute best advice in every situation because the student and the mentor have aligned interests. When the student makes money, the mentor makes money.

Let's discuss the elephant in the room, shall we? You are probably more than convinced by now that I am an extremely credible source for advice on real estate investing. But how can you be sure that the advice I am giving you in this book is good advice for you?

I make money when my students close deals, plain and simple. The only way for my students to close deals is to apply the right techniques and strategies. Therefore, this book has to be the absolute most accurate advice on real estate investing because my profits with my students depend on it. Some of the readers of this book will go on to work with my team and in order for us to produce the best results; they need to have the right education and the proper foundation. That is how all of my courses, articles and trainings have been created; with the end in mind. You're getting the best of the best in this book because of mutually aligned interests. My incentives to teach you are aligned with your aspirations to be a successful real estate investor.

Unfortunately, not everyone reading this will qualify for my apprentice program. We are a small team that can only work with a handful of people at any one time. Our focus is on quality, not quantity. We are looking for people who exhibit those character traits that we have found to produce extraordinary results, such as; honesty, trustworthiness, open-mindedness, coach ability and a strong desire to be a real estate investor. The good news is that you do have a leg up on the competition because you have purchased this book and have actually read it all the way to here! I want to encourage you to go to the special webpage I created just for readers of this book: **www.FreedomMentor.com/book**

You will have the opportunity to apply for my apprentice program there and our system will recognize that you are a "How to be a Real Estate Investor," book reader which will help you with your apprentice application. This is one of the many bonuses hidden in this book to help you become a successful investor.

Who is Your Mentor?

No successful person has ever done it alone. Every great individual in history has had a mentor. So often we see highly successful people in life and assume that they are self made. The truth is; no one is self made. Behind every successful person is a mentor, or mentors, that have inspired, coached and trained that person. Consequently, it's also the fastest shortcut to success. When you have a mentor, you reduce your learning curve by decades and put yourself light years ahead of where you would have been on your own. Successful real estate investors have mentors.

Like most important decisions, you must choose your mentors wisely, though. Oftentimes, new investors will align themselves with the first person they meet and the only thing worse than no mentor in real estate, is a bad one. Thankfully, determining the value of a mentor is not complicated. It is quite simple. As we discussed earlier on taking advice, you want to align yourself with people who are very successful and know far more than you do about the subject. You will be able to tell their value by what they have done personally in real estate and also who they have mentored before. In most cases, it's better to avoid the person who has never mentored someone before, even if they are extremely successful in their own right, because mentoring is a skill unto itself. You don't want to be someone's mentee guinea pig. Life's too short to be someone else's experiment. Go with the person who has a track record for mentoring others to success.

You'll need at least one mentor and the time to begin searching for that person is sooner rather than later.

Partners

A peculiar step some investors take when they first get started is adding on a partner to their fledgling endeavor. Perhaps new investors fear investing alone and want company? Maybe they assume the person they partner with brings tremendous value and is essential to the operation? Partners are very helpful in business, so long as you partner with the right people and you set up the partnership correctly.

First, you want to partner with someone for a definite period of time. Oftentimes, when two friends partner up in business, they do not set a specified time for their partnership and over time, when the inevitable happens and they each want the business to go in different directions, sadly they end up at odds with each other and the business falters. The way to eliminate that from the get-go is to have a specified ending point to the partnership.

Second, you should partner with someone who is providing tremendous value. The conflict that can most likely plague a partnership is when one partner is doing all the work and/or providing all the value and the other one is not pulling his/her weight. The way to eliminate this problem before it starts is to make sure that each partner is bringing value above and beyond simply working in the business. Further, defining the roles of each partner and what each person is responsible for is also very helpful.

With partnerships, you must begin with the end in mind. It may feel uncomfortable to start a relationship already thinking about what happens when it ends, but with business partnerships, that is exactly how you need to enter one.

What if you are already in a partnership right now as you are reading this? Make sure your partner is providing tremendous value. Put together a timeframe when the partnership could end and have a plan for who is responsible for what. If your partner will not participate in this exercise, you may have the wrong partner on your hands.

What's Your Investor IQ?

Congratulations! You now know how to think like a real estate investor. How would like to test your progress? How would like to determine your Investor IQ? I have created a fun and educational test that will help you gauge how well you think like an investor. This is another bonus for reading this book. To claim this bonus and determine your Investor IQ, go to: **www.FreedomMentor.com/book**

The 7 Habits of Highly Successful Investors

In addition to the important principles you discovered in this chapter, as well as the lessons revealed while assessing your Investor IQ, you also can download a special audio training called, "The 7 Habits of Highly Successful Real Estate Investors." Go to:

www.FreedomMentor.com/book

Part 3: Real Estate Investing 101

"Success is neither magical nor mysterious. Success is the natural
consequence of consistently applying the basic fundamentals."
—Jim Rohn

Are you certain that real estate investing is right for
you? Do you have a powerful and motivating *Why* that will
drive you to succeed? Are you confident you now know how
to think like a successful investor? Now you are ready for the
right real estate education. When the student is ready, the
teacher appears.

Real estate investing encompasses a vast ocean of information that can be very intimidating and extremely
difficult to consume all at the same time. The goal of this
section is to simplify the many different facets of real estate
investing and to show you how to understand such a large
topic quickly and easily.

To use a fishing analogy, when trout fishermen are trying to assess where the fish are located at on a very wide
river, they separate the wide river into many small streams.
Some parts of the river may be fast and shallow while others
slow and deep. Whereas looking at a very wide river can be
very intimidating and confusing, when mentally separated
into several small streams, evaluating the river and finding
the fish becomes much easier.

We're going to take that same approach here and segment real estate investing so that it is much easier for you to
understand the different facets, starting with the simplest
segmentation of all. The purpose of investing in real estate is
to make money and you make money in real estate either

now or later. Therefore, real estate investing can be summarized into two groups; fast cash techniques and wealth building strategies.

Fast cash, or making money now, provides you with cash in your pocket. For many people, extra money is very important to them right now. Wealth accumulation, or making money later, may provide cash flow and/or a big chunk of cash years into the future, which also has its own benefits. Most notably, making money later in real estate is usually very tax friendly. The IRS has enacted numerous provisions that can reduce the tax liabilities of cash later real estate profits.

A very important question to ask yourself is, "What do I want out of real estate?" If you are overflowing with liquid assets (cash) right now, either in a retirement account, an inheritance, a business you just sold or simply the steady accumulation of money overtime in a bank account, the prospects of having that money working for you in real estate in a very tax friendly way may be exactly what you want. Conversely, if you desperately need cash right now, maybe to stay afloat or to pay pressing bills, fast cash may be the smartest course of action for you. And in some cases, you may be in the middle of those two extremes and would like both, fash cash and wealth accumulation. Real estate can provide cash now, cash later or both.

> **WISDOM KEY:** The purpose of real estate investing is to create financial returns, plain and simple. Can your investing actions help people? Certainly! In fact, the way we teach investing is to always do deals that benefit all parties involved. Therefore, it should be a given that when you complete a transaction and make money, you are helping all parties involved.

The problem is that sometimes people get so caught up in doing, doing, doing, that they forget to make a profit. Sounds silly, doesn't it? It happens quite often. Whether you are going to make cash now, cash later or both, the purpose of real estate investing is to produce profits (this already assumes that every deal you do is a win-win-win.) Don't allow yourself to fall into the trap of being very active but producing very little economic results.

How to Make Fast Cash

Real estate provides several ways for you to create cash quickly. This section will describe the vast majority of ways to accomplish this. In many cases, you can generate this money without using your own cash or credit. Instead, the reason why you would make money in most situations is because you are putting a deal together or providing a service for a deal.

Plato said, "The beginning of knowledge is the definition of terms." Along with providing you with the techniques that produce cash for you right now, it's also important you understand how each is defined. The world of real estate has its own language and understanding real estate lingo will help you get a better picture of this whole business.

Flipping / Wholesaling / Buying and Re-selling

Although there are numerous terms or ways to describe this action, the concept is quite simple. When you flip, or wholesale, or buy and resell a property, what you are doing is getting a property owner to agree to sell you their property and then you are re-selling the property to a new buyer for more. The original owner signs a contract with you and then as soon as you have the deal *under contract* (whereby you have in writing, a contract stating the exact terms of the agreement), you then find a buyer who will pay more for the property than the agreement you have with the owner. You, then, make the money, or the spread, in the middle.

Although this is quite simple in concept, the actual process of how you get paid from this arrangement can be somewhat complicated at times. For example, once you have a contract in place between you and a property owner, instead of closing on the property the traditional way and then re-selling to another buyer, in certain situations, you can actually assign your contract to a new buyer. Then, at the closing, this new buyer will purchase the property from the original owner and you will step out of the way for an assignment fee.

In other scenarios, as in the case of some short sales (which will be discussed in detail later), you would first buy the property from the original owner, close on it using transactional funding, and then immediately re-sell the property to the new buyer. Both of these examples fall under this same category of flipping / wholesaling / buying and re-selling, but the way in which you obtained the spread, or the money in the middle, were quite different. The concept is simple but the way in which you get paid can be more complicated. To avoid confusion, focus on the concept for now.

The foundation for successfully applying this investing approach is being able to find properties that can be put under contract at an amount substantially lower than the current value (or with favorable terms). And the property must also be attractive enough to another buyer that he/she would be willing to pay you more for it than what you have it under contract for. When these two requirements are met, you can make very good money being the middle person and putting the deal together.

If you are getting paid to buy (or put under contract) a property for less than you can immediately re-sell it for, is that immoral, unethical or otherwise bad? Absolutely not! In fact, these deals can be an incredible win-win transaction for all parties involved given the right circumstances. But unfortunately, the word *flipping* has actually taken on a very negative connotation. In fact, the dreadful word *illegal* has actually been paired with *flipping*. To set the record straight, it's important to recognize that a large portion of the business world has functioned on the wholesale – retail model for centuries.

Real World Example: Look around your home at the many items you purchased from a retail store. The majority of those items wound up in your home from the following process: First, the manufacturer created items and sold them to a wholesaler. The manufacturer made a profit by charging more for the items than it cost him to manufacture them. Second, the wholesaler sold those exact same items to the retail store for more than what the wholesaler bought the items for from the manufacturer. The wholesaler made its profit by being the middleman; buying low and selling higher. Third, the retail store sold you the exact same items they bought from the wholesaler for more than what they paid. The retail store made their profit being the middleman and buying high and selling higher. Except for the manufacturer, everyone else made their money buying and re-selling the exact same item for more money to the next customer down the line.

Is it illegal to buy an item at one amount and then resell that same identical item for a larger amount? If it is, then the vast majority of businesses are built on an illegal wholesale-retail model. When you flip, or wholesale, or buy and resell real estate, you are operating under the same model that many of the most well respected businesses in history have operated. You are buying and then reselling an identical item for more money to the next customer down the line.

DISCLAIMER: On any legal related issues always consult a qualified attorney.

The reason why the word *illegal* appears in conjunction with the word *flipping* has to do with a very dishonest trick that unscrupulous people have been employing for a very long time. It is a dirty scam that involves re-selling a property to an unsuspecting buyer for far more than the property's true value.

Here is how the crime is conducted. First, an unscrupulous person finds an equally unscrupulous appraiser to appraise, or value, the property for far more than the true market value. Second, the unscrupulous person finds a naïve and unsuspecting buyer to purchase the property for an amount that is above-the true market-value. Third, the buyer obtains a loan that is based on the inflated and higher-than-true-value appraisal. Fourth, the buyer becomes the owner of a home that is worth far less than what he/she paid for it because the seller and the appraiser operated dishonestly.

That is where the word *flipping* got paired with *illegal*. It was originated from dishonest people selling real estate to a buyer for far more than its true market value. That is NOT the type of flipping we will be describing in this book. Instead, you will be learning how to morally, ethically and legally negotiate win-win transactions whereby you buy real estate at wholesale prices and sell them at true-market-value retail prices.

> **WISDOM KEY:** When dishonesty is introduced into any venture, trouble ensues. Therefore, be honest with all parties all the time. You will be far more successful being truthful anyway. One of the most infamous

mobsters in American history was Lucky Luciano. At the end of his life, while spending his last few breathes in a prison, when asked what he had learned from his life experiences, he said something along the lines of, "It took more work to make money dishonestly than it did to do it honestly. I wish I would have just done it right from the beginning."

In any real estate market, there are legitimate opportunities to get properties under contract at an amount less than the true market value. Here is a real world example, one of our students stumbled across a situation involving a very motivated seller. The owner of the property was about to lose her property to foreclosure in less than two months and she owed $50,000 on a home that could be valued at $150,000 or more once it was all fixed up. The owner didn't have the money to do any repairs and even worse, the tenants in the property would not allow her to show the property to perspective buyers so there were no real estate agents willing to help her.

Discouraged, this seller gave up and prepared for the worst possible outcome, foreclosure. Meanwhile, our student was marketing for motivated sellers and their advertisements caught the attention of this seller. Shortly after connecting, the two parties had a written agreement for our student to buy the property for $85,000. The seller was more than pleased with the agreed upon amount because the property was in such disrepair, all previous attempts to get help had failed and there was very little time left before it went to foreclosure.

Our student promptly marketed for an all cash investor buyer since the buyer had to be willing to purchase the property without a full and complete inspection due to the tenants not allowing anyone in the property. A local doctor and part-time investor was located who was willing to pay $100,000 cash and buy the property before the foreclosure.

Let's breakdown why this deal was a win-win transaction for all parties and why our student deserved a profit. Our student located a motivated seller that needed help. Other real estate professionals had turned her down when the seller had reached out for a solution. Our student solved the seller's problem. Further, our student found a buyer willing to purchase the property as-is (in its current condition of disrepair), prior to foreclosure for all cash. Finding that kind of buyer was something the seller did not know how to do. Our student deserved to earn a profit because she applied specific investing skills and knowledge to put together a win-win deal.

This deal exemplified how to do a win-win-win flip/wholesale/buy and resell transaction. Everyone in the deal benefited even though our student got the property under contract for less than the current market value. And moreover, our student didn't take advantage of the seller either. This person was in a real bind and other real estate professionals were unable to help her. Had it not been for our student, this seller would have gone into foreclosure. Instead, she had the ability to sell the property for $85,000, a full $35,000 above what she owed.

The fast cash approach to real estate investing allows you to make quick cash with the limited resources (no cash or credit required) and little or no risk (if the deal doesn't work out, you're not out anything). However, the profits are usually taxed more heavily than wealth building real estate income. Plus, in some cases, the profits can be slightly smaller than if you employ other techniques.

Flipping/wholesaling/buying and re-selling has been the foundation of many investor's careers. It is extremely popular, easy to get started with and can make you very, very wealthy if you do it over and over again.

Buying, Improving, Re-selling

This differs slightly, but significantly from the previous section because here, you are not only reselling the property for more than you bought it for, but you are also improving the property. This is what many people envision when they think of *real estate investing*. People often picture investing as purchasing a beat up, run down foreclosure, fixing it up until it sparkles and then re-selling to a first time home-buyer. This model has produced many millionaires throughout history and it will continue to because it works.

A very common example of this technique is that of a builder. The typical builder purchases a lot from a developer and then builds a property on that lot. Then, the builder re-sells the newly built property.

In fact, the developer is an example of this model as well. One approach that has created many real estate millionaires is to purchase raw land and then to improve it by adding roads and utilities, possibly having to change the zoning and then selling individual lots to builders. You may have heard the old saying, "The two most profitable businesses are buying whiskey by the bottle and selling it by the shot and buying real estate by the acre and selling it by the lot." Although this approach to real estate investing of buying, improving, then re-selling may sound wonderful, it has it's drawbacks too.

Improving real estate, whether it be turning raw land into buildable lots, empty lots into new built properties or rundown homes into renovated houses, involves far more risk and resources than flipping/wholesaling/buying and re-selling. First, money is required to purchase the un-improved property as well as to fund the improvement. Second, improving a property requires extensive specialized knowledge. Third, anytime you improve or build, most municipalities have rules that must be strictly adhered to in order to pass inspection. Fourth, a whole new level of liability is introduced when people are on the property working who may injure themselves while improving the property. Fifth, just because you improve the property does not mean the market is going to pay enough to compensate you for your improvement efforts. Developers are among the most at risk of such an outcome. Sometimes they make a gamble on a city growing in a certain direction only to see the population shift in an opposite direction just as they are finishing their development project. Therefore, improving a property as opposed to simply buying and re-selling a property without making any changes, is a significant responsibility.

But in some cases, with much risk comes much reward. For example, many builders make less than 10% profit on any one property. In isolation, that would appear risky, to put in all that time, effort and resources to build one property and get less than a 10% profit. Just a few mistakes and that profit could easily be eaten away. But most builders don't make their money on one deal; their money comes from the volume of properties. For example, if they build 500 homes in one subdivision, then 500 properties times 10% profit per $200,000 house equals $10,000,000. That's good money.

For a house renovater (or also referred to as a "rehabber"), someone who is going to turn an ugly house into a beautiful home, the typical minimum profit target is 20%. This is substantially more than you will usually make simply wholesaling or flipping a property without doing any improvement to the property. To profit 20% on a $200,000 house is $40,000. That's good money.

For a developer, they may purchase farm land at $10,000 per acre and then sell off 4 lots per acre at $20,000 a piece. Assuming some expense for land improvement, this example still yields a huge return.

In each of these cases, by taking on the risk of improving the property can bring a much more substantial reward.

Most investors do not start with this investing approach due to the capital and skill level required. Some progress to it, while others choose to stay away and continue to make their money being purely a middleman. However, some people have extensive experience in building or renovating and therefore would far prefer this approach over simply being a flipper/wholesaler.

> **WISDOM KEY:** When in comes to deciding whether to make some money now or far more money later, my philosophy is that a quick nickel beats a slow dime.

The most successful investors are flexible and allow each deal to dictate the best course of action for the most profit. Oftentimes with really good deals, you will have the option to either earn a smaller amount quickly by selling immediately without improving the property or take on the risk and resources outlay required to renovate the property for a bigger profit down the road.

> **Real World Example:** One of our students found a really beat up home in a not-so-good neighborhood. The seller had moved out months prior and vandals

had further trashed the home which was already in serious disrepair. Our student got a contract in place with the sellers at a price of $55,000. It needed about $20,000 to bring it up to the level that a retail home buyer would want to purchase it and move in. Judging by what the other homes in the area had recently sold for, it appeared $130,000 would be a possible sales price but more realistically, it would probably sell to a new buyer at $120,000.

This student had a number of investor buyers come by and most offered between $55,000 and $60,000 for the deal. As investor buyers often do, they made our student feel like the home would require $40,000 to fix up and would only sell for $100,000 (An example of asking the barber if you need a haircut.) When attempting to re-sell a property to an investor buyer, it is common for the prospective buyer to point out the negatives of a property in an attempt to negotiate a lower price.

Our student was wise and didn't succumb to this negative feedback. Instead, he sought out the opinions of a few hard money lenders, people who lend money to investors to fix up property. The hard money lenders all liked the deal and therefore our student decided to borrow the money and fix up the deal himself, weathering the potential risks in search of more than the measly $5,000 profit he would have gathered had he immediately resold it to an investor buyer.

It took a few months longer than he would have liked, 6 months altogether, from start to finish, but his profit ended up being just under $25,000. His biggest mistake turned out to be that his initial asking price of

$130,000 was too high and had he listed it at $120,000 from the beginning, he would have found a buyer immediately and the deal would have closed in less than 4 months. However, he was still really happy and made a great profit for his efforts; far more money than if he would have simply resold it to another investor buyer. *In this case a slow quarter beat a quick nickel!*

When you take on the higher level of risk and responsibility to actually improve a property, you can potentially make more money than by simply re-selling it. Also, in some cases, a deal will only make money if you improve it so you won't have the option to immediately re-sell it anyways. The drawbacks are that money is required to purchase the unimproved property and to fund the improvement. Specific knowledge about renovating/building is required and knowledge of codes and zoning is necessary. Plus, there is more liability involved. But with much risk can come much reward.

WISDOM KEY: Some may assume that simply having a *good contractor* will bridge the knowledge gap necessary to improve real estate. Experience has taught us that a *good contractor* is only as good as the person who hires him/her. Herein lies another reason why you need to make sure you align yourself with mentors that can bridge the knowledge gaps for you. Renovating, improving or building a home is a whole lot more technical than simply hiring good contractors to do the work. Oftentimes, asking a contractor about a project is like asking a barber if you need a

haircut. His opinion may be biased toward him getting paid to do the work.

Commissions / Fees

The final technique that can bring you cash now in real
estate is through commissions or fees. In most cases, you will
need to have a license in order to collect this money. Real
Estate Agents typically make a 3% commission when they
either represent a buyer or a seller in a transaction. That
commission percentage can really add up fast and there are
many agents that make 7 figures per year.

For some strange reason, as a general rule, the real estate investing community has balked at the idea of investors
having a real estate license. They usually site issues about
how it limits and restricts an investor's options. On the
contrary, having a real estate license is like having a license
to print money. Sure, it does hold you to a higher standard in
your business practices, but isn't that the kind of business
person you want to be anyways? Being held to a higher
standard is a great thing for honest people. You can get more
money from each closing by not giving that money away to
an agent. You can have that commission money come back to
you.

Real World Example: Here's an example of where
an investor can earn extra money from a commission
or fee. One of our students had been investing for
sometime and most of the people around him, friends
and family included, thought he was a real estate
agent. He happened to have his license but had never
operated as a traditional agent. A friend approached
him and asked if he could help him buy his first

> house. Since our student had bought numerous properties over the years, he thought it would be a good way to help his friend out and make a little money for the effort. His friend purchased a $350,000 house and our student earned a 3% commission, or $10,500. It only used up a few hours of his time and he helped his friend buy their first home wisely. As you can see, commission income can be a very profitable addition to your investing endeavors.

The drawback to having a real estate license is the expense and time associated with obtaining and maintaining one. It's not cheap. By the time you finish the testing, the continuing education, the E&O insurance, the Realtor® dues, etc, it costs thousands of dollars and consumes large amounts of time to be a licensed agent. The benefit is that you can earn commissions on all the deals you are already doing (more profit per deal) and you can earn commissions on deals that don't fit as an investing type deal. Plus, you get access to your local Multiple Listing Service (MLS) system which allows you access to the most important database in real estate. Unfortunately, only real estate agents are allowed full access to the coveted MLS system.

So you may be asking yourself, "should I go get my license?" The answer is; it depends. For most people, the plan should be to go make some money in real estate investing first and then consider getting your real estate license using some of the profits. If you have a license in retirement already, you may be able to file one document and pay a small fee and you are an active agent again. If getting your license out of retirement is that easy, you may want to re-activate. Otherwise, be patient with taking on such a huge commitment as getting your license until you have made some money and experienced real estate investing first hand.

There are other ways to earn fees or commissions besides being a real estate agent too. Some investors are also appraisers, or inspectors, or mortgage brokers. All of these professions can be great ways to put cash in your pocket from real estate.

You may even be able to simply send the contact information of potentially motivated sellers to other investors or agents and get a small fee for passing along the data, also referred to as "bird dogging". Bird-dogging is when someone finds a good real estate deal and rather than getting it under contract, they simply send the information along to an investor or agent who handles the deal from there. The business plan of a bird-dog is to simply send along a name and number, or an address, to a more experienced real estate profession in exchange for a small marketing fee. It can be a great way to earn quick money in real estate with little or no experience.

However, the marketing expertise required to find highly motivated sellers is oftentimes more difficult than negotiating a deal and getting a property under contract. Therefore, in most cases, a bird dog can earn far more money by simply taking the extra time to educate him/herself on how to negotiate with seller, what contracts to use and how to complete them properly. Instead of making a few bucks as a bird dog, the extra effort to get the deal under contract could be the difference between a few hundred dollars and a few thousand dollars.

Earning commissions and fees in real estate can be a great way to add extra cash to your pocket. The only drawbacks, in most cases, is the time and money required to obtain and maintain the proper licenses.

Those are the three ways people make fast cash in real estate. You can buy and resell a property with no improvement, you can buy, improve and then resell or you can make a fee or commission. Now let's turn to how you can build long term wealth through real estate.

How to Build Long Term Wealth

Real estate is not only a fabulous vehicle for putting money in your pocket now. It can also create long term financial security. In fact, this is what real estate is known for, building long term wealth. As you have already learned, the majority of wealth is stored in real estate. In this section, you'll learn how you can build your financial empire from real estate.

Buy and Hold

This is the technique most associated with real estate investing. The concept of this approach is that you purchase real estate and then rent it out to tenants. This is sometimes referred to as *traditional buy and hold investing*. It has been the source of incredible wealth. Anyone who has played the board game Monopoly knows the power of owning and leasing out real estate. And as mentioned earlier, this technique can be extremely tax friendly and therefore you are able to keep more of what you earn than with the fast cash approach shared in the previous section.

There are three majors profit centers from buying and holding real estate. First, if the tenant pays you more than your costs (mortgage payment, taxes, insurance, maintenance, etc), you profit from a monthly cash flow. Second, your mortgage payment may include a principle component so each time a payment is made, the tenant is actually paying down the mortgage balance on the property and thereby increasing your equity. Third, in most areas, over a long period of time, real estate appreciates in value, so you profit from the increase in value of the property.

> **WISDOM KEY:** A noted Yale economist conducted a study of real estate in America from 1900 to 2000 and discovered that adjusted for inflation residential real estate does not appreciate in value. His shocking research points out that residential real estate only keeps pace with inflation, as a general rule. In fact, sometimes, real estate doesn't even keep pace with inflation. Case in point, Baytown, TX. In 1981, you could have purchased a single family home on Lariat Dr in Baytown, TX for $80,000. Thirty years later, you could purchase a home on Lariat Dr in Baytown, TX for you guessed it, $80,000. The price didn't increase in over 30 years, even though a dollar was worth far less 30 years later. Surprising, isn't it? The fact is, real estate is extremely localized and every neighborhood behaves differently. Even during a booming market, certain neighborhoods may be struggling. And during a down market, certain neighborhoods may be booming. When it comes to determining which areas will appreciate, the lesson is, *location, location, location.*

The secret to successfully applying the buy and hold strategy is to buy the property below true value so that you have instant equity and then to profit from the cash flow and the principle pay down. Appreciation should be a bonus and an *icing on the cake.* It should not be the reason for the investment. Most investors are unaware of this and therefore, many have lost their shirts on real estate investments that they purchased in the hopes of profiting from appreciation. This is also referred to as *speculation.*

The other issue investors have voiced as it pertains to buying and holding real estate is in being a landlord. Some even associate, *unclogging toilets at 3AM* with land lording.

However, not all people dread property management. In fact, property management has been deemed as one of the most profitable businesses in America (based on almost any measure of profitability). Property management is a challenge if there is not a system in place to handle every issue that comes up and/or if the property does not cash flow strong enough to warrant the expenses associated with leasing. But, property management can also be quite lucrative.

> **Real World Example:** One of our students has a property that will sell for about $125,000 in today's market. It leases for $1000 per month. The amount owed on the property is about $100,000. The total monthly payment is $800. This $800 payment includes principle, interest, taxes, insurance and MI (mortgage insurance). The positive cash flow is therefore $200 ($1000 Rental Income - $800 Expenses). Property management companies usually charge 10% of rental income (as well as 1/3 of the first month's rent when a new tenant is moved into the property.) If our student turned this property over to a property management firm, he would pay $100 per month for their services (or 50% of the total cash flow). That would leave $100 per month positive cash flow. Here you see why property management firms can be extremely profitable. 10% of the gross rental income can represent a huge percentage of the overall profit of the deal.

Enlisting a property management firm can be a wise decision. They usually have a very good leasing system already in place on how to manage properties. They usually have relationships with vendors like eviction attorneys and maintenance men who are needed to run a great management system. And they typically can handle all the issues and calls from tenants, even at 3AM in the morning.

The drawbacks with hiring a property management company can be that they charge 10% of the gross rental income, which can account for a large percentage of your positive cash flow. Also, not every property management company is created equal and some do not have a good leasing system in place.

Further, and most insidious of all property management company hiring challenges, is when the company profits from repairs. Sometimes, the contractor doing the work may provide the property management company referral fees for the work they are given. This incentivizes the property management company to come up with work to be done to the property. Since you as the owner pay all the bills for maintenance, there is no real downside to having you pay for more work. In fact, the more maintenance is done, the easier it will be to lease and for the property management company to collect 10% of gross. They get 10% of gross and they don't have to pay for any of the repairs of the asset, but instead they may *get* paid as a result of more maintenance!

For some investors who have hired and subsequently fired their property manager, this one detail was the cause for the dismissal. Ultimately, these investors learned that since the property management firm benefited from a property's need for repairs, the property management firm would not be incentivized to bring in a high quality tenant who wouldn't destroy the place. Sadly, the more a tenant was likely to trash a property, the more potential revenue that property management company could earn from that deal.

How does a property management company have the ability to move a bad tenant into a property? Most property managers send rental applications of prospective tenants to the owner for final review. As a way to control what the owner has to choose from, some property management firms have been known to only produce one or two potential tenant candidates. This forces the property owner to make a choice between a bad tenant and a bad tenant. Next, the property owner typically asks the property manager if the tenant is good or not. Herein lies another example of asking the barber if you need a haircut. The problem is, what may be a good tenant to a property owner may be a bad tenant to a property manager. Because when you factor in the 1/3 of the first month's rent for re-leasing, it can actually behoove the property management company to continue to re-lease the property. Unfortunately, the financial incentives for a property management company can sometimes be at odds with a property owner.

Should a property management firm be hired to manage your property? In the previous real world example, our student actually manages his own property. Why? First, this student has a very solid property management system already established, from how to locate quality tenants quickly, to how to handle 3AM toilet clogging calls. Second, all of the vendors needed to run a great management system are already in place for him, from the eviction attorney to the maintenance person. Therefore, it is worth $100 per month for the student to manage the property without paying a management firm.

However, there are excellent property management firms out there. If the property is located far from the owner, the property owner does not have their system and/or if there is no team in place, it is far better to have a property management company. The best of all worlds is a property management company that you manage who follows your system and uses your team members! To learn more about building your team, see Appendix B.

Buying and holding real estate differs greatly between different types of properties as well. Single family homes can be very easy to re-sell if a tenant moves out and you want to realize your equity profits. However, leasing single family homes can be costly if the tenant stops paying or the property goes vacant because you have no way of offsetting the vacancy and therefore, incur heavy vacancy holding costs until the property is re-leased.

Income producing properties like duplexes (2 units), triplexes (3 units), quads (4 units), on up to apartment buildings have more units to off set your monthly expenses in the event of a vacancy. However, income producing properties can be more difficult to sell and may not gain in value as rapidly. The reason is that income producing properties are typically valued based on how much income they produce, whereas single family homes are valued based on what the market will pay for them. Single family homes are the most desirable residential properties, have the largest potential buyer pool and usually gain in value better than income producing properties. Rental rates, in general, do not rise as quickly as home prices can. So some investors favor buying and holding only single family homes because of the bigger cash payouts they receive when they re-sell.

Income producing property investors opt for the steady cash flow even during the low vacancy times as well as the ability to offset any unit vacancies with other rented units. As you invest, you will find which niche you would rather focus your energies on. Oftentimes, investors own both single family homes and income producing properties as well. Some even graduate to owning larger apartment buildings due to the economies of scale that are created from numerous units all contained in the same place with a full time, onsite manager. One of the great benefits of owning an apartment building above a certain size is the ability to hire an onsite manager to handle everything. As opposed to paying 10% per unit, you can actually put the person on salary and obtain terrific service for far less total capital outlay.

But, the potential downside to putting all of your eggs into one basket is if that basket fails, the results can be devastating. Using 1031 exchanges, an ambitious investor will trade up their single family homes, duplexes, and quads into one large apartment building. At first, all is good. Then, as can happen in business, things change, and their apartment building begins to stop producing. Their basket begins to fail. Since this investor has all of his/her eggs in one basket, his/her long term financial security ebbs and flows by the behavior of their one property. What's the lesson? Try to avoid putting all of your eggs in one basket.

WISDOM KEY: There is another set of expenses that must be calculated when evaluating any buy and hold deal, whether it be a single family home or a large apartment building...maintenance. The reality is that real estate deteriorates over time. As you know, the IRS allows you to depreciate an equal amount over the course of time to account for deterioration. That is certainly a gift considering most buildings are built to last far longer than the IRS allows investors to depreciate. But many parts of a property are not built to last long term. Roofs usually only last 10 to 15 years, depending on the material and the location (the desert is really harsh on comp roofs which is why you often see clay roofs in places like Las Vegas). HVAC systems usually last 7 to 10 years before some part or all of the system fails and tenants that forget to change the HVAC filters can shorten that life expectancy even more. Hot water heaters may last 7 years, if you're lucky. Carpets and floor coverings oftentimes have to be replaced every time a tenant moves out, even if they have only lived in the property for a year or less. Depending on how rough the tenant lived in your property, new interior paint may have to be added every few years too. Therefore, you must account for the costs of maintenance when evaluating the cash flow of a buy and hold investment.

The key to successfully owning and holding real estate is to be very selective in the properties you purchase. If you buy the property right and manage it correctly, it can be a rich and rewarding investment. If you buy the property wrong or manage it poorly, it can be a difficult and frustrating experience.

Some experts have said that even if you buy real estate wrong, given enough time, even a bad investment can correct itself. As you learned from the Yale professor and from the example of Baytown, TX, that is not always true. When you have access to people who have experienced a lifetime of real estate ownership lessons, you can make more informed decisions and ultimately, be more successful.

WISDOM KEY: The main reason why some buy and hold deals are not profitable can be linked to the financing on the property. The financing is a very important component of a buy and hold investment. Sometimes you can even purchase the property with very little instant equity but if the loan terms are right, it can be a terrific investment. Case in point; if you paid $190,000 for a $200,000 property but the seller provided the financing of $190,000 at 0% interest for 30 years, every payment would go directly towards the principal and soon, you would have tremendous equity and hopefully very strong cash flow. Another example would be if you didn't originate any new money to purchase the property, but instead, simply began making payments on the seller's existing mortgage, you could become the owner of the property and actually leave the seller's mortgage in place. This is a strategy known as "Subject To" and investors have been employing this concept for a very long time with great success. The loan usually has a lower interest rate than most investors could obtain by originating a new non-owner occupied loan and also, it's not in the investor's name. You'll learn more about creative finance techniques such as these in a later section.

The government can actually be a landlord's best friend in certain situations too. Section 8 is a program that is linked to welfare whereby the government may pay the property owner partial and/or the complete rental payment each month. As of this writing, the government has not gone broke yet and therefore pays each month, on time. With Section 8 (and any of its local derivatives), the government pays a standard amount per number of bedrooms the property has. In some cases, the tenant has to come up with part of the monthly rent, but in other cases, the government pays the entire amount.

For most property owners of Section 8 housing, the government supplying the entire monthly payment is ideal. The Section 8 department has a strict set of standards that the property must adhere to in order to be eligible for the program. Once a property is eligible to accept Section 8 tenants, it allows the owner to rest easy since Uncle Sam will be paying the rent on time each month (so long as those government issued checks are good and don't bounce due to insufficient funds). Section 8 can be a terrific option for investors who want the benefits of long term buying and holding without the headaches of worrying about their rent payment each month.

With all the apparent benefits, as always, there are a few drawbacks. First, maintenance on Section 8 properties can be an issue since the tenant is not very motivated to keep up the property. Especially if the government is paying the entire monthly payment, the tenant has no vested interest in the property. Second, as the old Chinese proverb states, "those in the free seats hiss first." As counter-intuitive as this may sound, the less someone pays, the more they complain, as a general rule in business. As it relates to property man-agement, a person who pays $8,000/mo in rent for a luxury home will usually give a landlord far less grief than a Section 8 tenant who has the government pay the $800/mo for their 3 bedroom home. Section 8 property management is most likely to generate the dreaded call at 3AM from a tenant that needs a small, petty problem fixed. The solution is a great property management system. It is also vitally important that a Section 8 investor fully understand the rules, regula-tions and details about the local Section 8 program where the property is located since it can vary from state to state and even from county to county. Government subsidized housing has the great benefit of almost guaranteed income but the drawback of increased management requirements.

Buy/Control and Rent to Own / Sell on Terms

Real estate investors have strived to minimize the risks associated with *traditional buy and hold investing* while still sharing in the benefits. In other words, they have sought to have their cake and eat it too. What they wanted was a tenant that would be ultra motivated to keep up the payments on time each month and would also handle and pay for every maintenance problem that arose. Thus was born the creative investing techique known as *sell on terms, rent to own* or *lease with an option to buy*.

Selling a property on this "rent to own" basis is rarely employed on income producing properties and is therefore most popular with single family homes. The tenant is referred to as a "tenant buyer" and what makes this type of renter different is that they are no longer just a tenant. They are now going to be the owner someday and therefore, hypothetically, they should be more likely to make their monthly payments on time and to cover any maintenance issues that may spring up.

There are many ways in which this concept is executed. Some investors actually sell the property to the tenant buyer and the investor actually becomes the bank and collects mortgage payments. Other investors remain the owner of the property and simply lease the property to the tenant buyer along with providing the tenant with an option to purchase the property for a year or two. Still other investors take this whole concept one step further and instead of buying the real estate, they actually lease with option to buy the real estate from the original owner and then re-lease the property to another tenant buyer, oftentimes referred to as a *sandwich lease option*. Each state has different laws as it pertain to these concepts so what works in one state may not work in another. But rather than get bogged down with the details of creative financing (we'll do that in the next chapter), the key here is to recognize the concept. Instead of just leasing the property to a tenant, you obtain a tenant buyer who wants to purchase the home. The difference is subtle, but can be very effective.

The profit centers with this technique may include all of those included in traditional buy and hold investing as well as the ability to obtain an upfront non-refundable option payment from the tenant when they first move in (as opposed to a refundable deposit) or a down payment if the house is being sold on terms. Plus, you have the ability to get a big profit at the end of the option period if the tenant buyer actually buys the home.

Many rehabbers have been known to employ a combination of the buy, renovate and re-sell technique with this sell on a rent to own basis technique. There are three reasons why this is a good financial combination. First, you can sell a property for a higher price when you are offering favorable terms to a buyer than you could on the open market to a buyer who is getting their own loan. Second, you may not have to pay any sales commissions that are normally charged when you sell a home on the open market which can save you 6%. And third, if the property is held for a least 1 year, as of this writing, currently, the IRS considers the profit to fall under the category of long term capital gains as opposed to ordinary income which can save a tremendous amount in tax liability.

With all of these benefits though, there must be some drawbacks, right? For die hard buy and hold investors, they will argue that if you sell a property, you forever give up the opportunity to profit from that asset. However, seasoned creative real estate investors would counter that argument by pointing out that less than 20% of all tenant buyers ever exercise their option to buy the home. Therefore, the property is actually rarely sold when offered on a rent to own.

In addition, for any property other than a single family home, this approach can be difficult to apply because apartment dwellers rarely want to become the owner of an apartment building. Also, some investors would make the point that people actually treat their own stuff worse than the stuff they borrow from others. Meaning, if you let a tenant think *they own the place*, they may actually tear it up more than if they thought it was a rental.

Outside of these objections, offering your property on a rent to own to a tenant buyer can oftentimes bring you the best of all long term wealth building worlds.

Although there are creative ways to curb some of the inherent risks in owning real estate, at the end of the day, you are still dealing with people and people don't always follow through with their promises. Unlike the fast cash approach to investing whichs allow you to get in and get out, when you acquire real estate you are taking on an important responsibility. If the tenant or tenant buyer does not follow through with their promises, you are still responsible for keeping up the payments and the maintenance of the property.

It has been said that sometimes, it is a whole lot easier to get into a real estate deal than it is to get out of one. The way to minimize your exposure to problems is to be selective and only acquire deals that have lots of room for error. Meaning, they have tons of instant equity, the potential for terrific cash flow, very favorable financing terms or all three.

Many people have built their fortune from buying and leasing real estate and it could be your key to financial freedom. But it also has its own set of challenges that you need to account for in your endeavors.

Ambitious people can sometimes be in a hurry for success and they attribute reaching their goals to owning more real estate. The goal should not be to simply own more real estate, but instead, to own solid real estate investments. It is better to own less and own right than own more and have made poor buying decisions. Patiently and wisely build your real estate portfolio. It'll pay dividends for generations.

Part 4: Advanced Investing Techniques

"Education is the most powerful weapon which you can use to change the world." – Nelson Mandela

Now that you understand the basics of how money is made with real estate, now it's time to get a far deeper understanding of the subject. There are several specific techniques that can be applied, depending on the situation. The goal of this section is to introduce you to these different strategies and how to apply them in the real world.

Wholesaling

Wholesaling is the single most popular strategy among those who are just getting started investing in real estate. The reason is that it requires little to no resources, responsibilities or commitments and it can generate quick cash. Also known as "flipping", the concept of wholesaling is that you are getting a seller to agree to a low price or favorable terms and then you are wholesaling, or flipping, the deal to a new buyer for a higher price or fee.

The traditional wholesale transaction looks something like this: a homeowner agrees to sell their home for $200,000 even though the retail value may be $275,000. Then, as soon as the wholesaler has the deal locked up with a contract, the wholesaler then finds an investor willing to pay more than $200,000, say $210,000 or $215,000. Then, at the closing, the wholesaler makes the spread of $10,000 –to $15,000.

The general rule of thumb that has been established with this model is that wholesalers need to find real estate deals at 65% of true market value (or less is even better) and then flip to investors who will purchase that same property for around 70% of value. That presupposes two very important events; one, that there are real estate owners out there willing to sell their property for 65% of value (or less) and two, that there are investor buyers out there willing to pay 70% of value for real estate. In the real world, real estate owners willing to sell their properties for 65% or less of value encompass a very, very small percentage of the total number of sellers. And the numbers get increasingly smaller as you move into areas with higher prices, areas with nicer properties and areas with newer built real estate. On the other hand though, the number of potential wholesale deals increases dramatically as you move into lower priced, older and rougher areas of town.

Why? First, newer built homes, for the most part, lack enough equity to allow for a wholesaler to pick up a deal at 65 cents on the dollar because most have mortgages against the property that are nearly equal to the value.

Second, as property prices increase, the ability to maintain the same percentages becomes increasingly difficult. For example, 65% of $100,000 is $65,000 while 65% of $1,000,000 is $650,000. It becomes more and more difficult to maintain such favorable percentages as the price increases.

Third, nicer areas of town are usually in greater demand and therefore finding buyers is not nearly as difficult, regardless of the property's condition. Most sellers of properties in nice areas can simply list the property with a local real estate agent on the Multiple Listing Service (MLS) and if priced right, will sell very quickly.

Fourth, nicer properties tend to be easier to sell and most owners of great condition properties are not as willing to give up their property for such a low price.

Fifth, as a gross generalization, higher priced and nicer area property owners tend to have access to more information and resources and typically have the wherewithal to get a property marketed correctly so that they can sell for more than 65% of value. Unlike at any other time in history, real estate owners can now go onto the internet and with a few key strokes, they can find out approximately what their property is worth, making it that much harder for wholesalers to find deals at 65 or less cents on the dollar. Therefore, wholesale deals tend to be found in the older and/or lower priced and/or rougher parts of town and the more in disrepair the property is, the more likely the owner may be willing to give up their property on the cheap.

An ethical issue exists with wholesaling that is rarely talked about or mentioned. Sometimes, the only reason why wholesalers are able to get a property under contract for 65% of true value or less is because the owner doesn't know any better or has an inaccurate understanding of what the value of their property really is. Are you really helping a seller if you are getting them to agree to 65% or less of value when you know in your heart that they are unaware of what they actually have on their hands? This is an ethical question that you may have to confront in your investing endeavors. The reality is that for most real estate owners can simply call up a real estate agent and if that agent spends the time it takes to get the property marketed on the MLS properly, most sellers can get at least 80% of value. And in some cases, 90%+ on the open market.

Some investors take the stance that, "if the seller is happy with what I've offered, then a deal is a deal." Other investors think, "If I know that this seller could simply put this property on the MLS and make $25,000 more than selling it to me for 65 cents on the dollar, then I need to at least share this information with the seller so that they can make a more informed decision."

In addition to the ethical issues, there are practical issues that can be argued on both sides as well. The drawback of not educating the seller of all of their options, such as putting the property on the MLS with an agent, is that after the contract is signed, they may begin asking friends and family about their decision. Soon the owner may realize, even before you've closed, that they are selling their property for far less than they should. Their next move will be to try to get out of their contract with you by any means necessary (legal or otherwise). When a person thinks they are being taken advantage of, as you learned from the pain and pleasure lesson, they will go to great lengths to get things straightened out.

However, by educating a seller on how they can possibly get much more for their deal than you are offering, you may lose the deal altogether. Proponents of educating property owners of their options would also argue that some sellers will actually appreciate the information and then still end up agreeing to work with you to avoid any future hassles with real estate agents or other people viewing the property. In such cases, you can feel good that you did provide the seller with many options and if they chose to sell to you, even though you were offering less, it's more likely they won't back out before it closes and all parties will be happy. For our students, we strongly recommend they provide property owners with all of their options and then allow the sellers to make the choice that is best for them.

> **WISDOM KEY:** Always do the right thing in business and operate in such a manner that if your actions were ever recorded on the front page of the newspaper, you would feel good about the story written about you.

You can wholesale all types of real estate, from houses to commercial shopping centers. However, certain properties create terrific little niches for the traditional wholesale strategy. One great niche involves wholesaling vacant lots. There are always local builders looking to pickup vacant lots to build on. Since the property is very simple with very few variables (zoning and if it has power, water and sewer going to it), vacant lots can be among the fastest and simplest traditional wholesales you can do. Plus, the person you are trying to sell to won't easily get connected to the owner because most people don't live on a vacant lot. (A real problem for wholesalers is when the new buyer gets in direct contact with the original seller thereby removing the middleman, the wholesaler).

Another great wholesale niche involves older vacant homes in areas where there are many tear downs and new luxury homes being built. Luxury home builders may be buying properties for $200,000 and then bulldozing the existing structure and building $2,000,000 luxury castles on the lot. Once again, a vacant property makes wholesaling so much easier.

A third terrific wholesale niche involves older homes in an area that is being revitalized. You can spot these areas easily by looking for a disproportionately large number of dumpsters in the drive ways of vacant homes in the neighborhood. That will indicate that rehabbers have moved into that area and are vigorously buying up older homes and renovating them into more modern residences that bring a much higher price than the neighborhood used to bring. With this niche, it really pays to know where the *next big area* is going to be so that you can get there before *everybody knows about it*. As you can see, certain niches are ideal for traditional wholesaling.

> **Real World Example:** One of our students received a call from a property owner who needed some quick cash. He had a small vacant lot situated in a nice neighborhood that he had owned for sometime. The reason for the vacancy was that he had moved his mobile home to his farm in the country years prior. This vacant lot owner was in a hurry and without any negotiation, said he only wanted $6,000 for the property. Our student promptly drove to meet the owner immediately and within the hour had a contract tp buy the lot for $6,000. Our student then put the property on the MLS (check your local MLS policies and procedures because not all allow investors to list properties that they do not own) and had a buyer the next day for $18,000. Start to finish, the entire deal closed in 20 days and the profit was nearly $10,000. That's what a traditional wholesale looks like when everything goes smoothly.

In the end, traditional wholesaling is all about getting to a deal before anyone else knows about it, getting it under contract and then getting a buyer as fast as possible to buy it. When all the pieces of this puzzle come together, these can be very profitable deals and the money can flow in very quickly.

Retail Wholesales

The retail wholesale is a phrase coined by our team to describe when you flip or wholesale a property to a retail buyer. The traditional wholesale typically involves selling the property to another investor buyer. There certainly are instances where this is the most profitable option. Usually when the property is in complete disrepair with fix up tasks far exceeding simple cosmetic work or if the property is vacant land as in the case of the example above.

Our team discovered that oftentimes you could retail wholesale a deal to a retail buyer and make 10 times as much in profits for the same amount of work as traditionally wholesaling it to an investor buyer. Most people would actually be surprised to discover that some retail buyers are not picky and can be very flexible with property condition issues. In fact, some retail buyers actually enjoy painting and doing light, cosmetic fix up projects to a home they just purchased. Further, some motivated sellers own properties in perfect or near perfect condition as well. Thus was born the retail wholesale strategy, whereby you flip the property the same way as a traditional wholesale but your buyer is a person who is going to move into the property (a retail buyer), creating far larger profits than selling to an investor buyer.

Another advantage of having this investing technique in your tool belt is that some deals will not have enough equity to make money as a traditional wholesale but may still have enough as a retail wholesale. For example, let's say the home has a value of $400,000 but the borrower owes $350,000. Although there is some equity, there is not enough for an investor buyer to pay cash for the house and still leave room for a wholesaler to make any money. Remember the 65%

rule? 65% of $400,000 is $260,000. In this instance, a retail wholesale may be the ideal strategy. The concept is that you are contracting to buy the property for one price and then selling the property to another buyer for a higher price. However, in many cases, as opposed to assigning the contract to the new buyer, with a retail wholesale you conduct two separate closings, or what is also called a concurrent closing or a back to back closing.

Both traditional wholesale and retail wholesale deals can be true no cash, no credit investing transactions. Most purported *no cash, no credit* investing strategies actually contain hidden places where real money is required. But with both of these techniques, you may be able to only put down $1 earnest money when the contract with the seller is executed and you may not incur any other expenses out of pocket after that. You can literally make a fortune with no cash or no credit buying and selling real estate through wholesaling.

A retail wholesale can earn you 10+ times as much as a traditional wholesale. Whereas you might get $3,000 assigning your contract to an investor buyer, you may be able to earn $30,000 or more by selling to a retail buyer. But with the increased in economic opportunity comes a far more detailed and potentially complicated transaction. The main reason is that retail buyers typically use standard mortgage loans to purchase property and the underwriting guidelines of some of these loans can be quite stringent. In an attempt to curb illegal flipping, some underwriting guidelines have not only stopped illegal flipping in its tracks but it has also prevented legitimate flipping from taking place as well. As you'll discover later, having the right mortgage person on your team will be vital to you successfully completing a retail wholesale.

> **Real World Example:** A homeowner that had just relocated approached one of our students with a request to purchase his home for $90,000. The home needed a little work, it was vacant and the seller just wanted out. He owed about $50,000 so he was more than pleased to get nearly $40,000 in his pocket. Meanwhile, our student recognized that the home could sell for as much as $130,000 if he just did a few quick cosmetic improvements, such as patch a small roof leak, clean the carpet and thoroughly clean everything else. After getting the deal under contract for $90,000, our student invested less than $500 to quickly make those improvements and immediately put the property on the MLS. He had a buyer quickly and ended up selling it for $120,000. At the closing, our student used transactional funding to purchase the property from the seller for $90,000 and then the next day, re-sold the property to the new buyer for $120,000. After closing costs and commissions, our student earned more than $20,000. xcept for the $500 to make a few improvements, our student used no cash or credit and made a very sizable profit.

Options

Very similar to both traditional and retail wholesaling is optioning real estate. With an option, you are getting an owner to provide you with an option to purchase their property. This is basically the same thing as when you execute a purchase contract with an owner to sell you their property. The main difference with an option is that it usually lasts for a much longer period of time (sometimes years) than the typical purchase contract (usually 30 to 60 days). Much like a wholesale deal, the option investor can then either assign the option contract to another buyer or buy the property and re-sell it or of course, buy the property and hold onto it. Options are often used in commercial deals since they usually take a whole lot longer to close than a residential deal.

Real World Example: Aristotle Onassis, one of the world's greatest entrepreneurs once said, "The secret to business is to know something that nobody else knows." Here's an example of getting to a spot before anyone else knows about it. In Middle Tennessee, just south of Nashville, sits what used to be the sleepy farming community of Spring Hill. One ambitious option investor caught wind that General Motors was going to be building a gigantic manufacturing facility in Spring Hill. He immediately took up residence at the local Holiday Inn and for a few weeks proceeded to contact and meet with every farmer he could, offering them an outrageous amount per acre for their land. He tied up these farmers with simple option contracts that expired after 1 year. The farmers thought he was the out-of-town fool willing to pay double for their land and these farmers thought they were taking advantage of him. Right on schedule, GM moved in and began buying up land for the enormous vehicle manufacturing plant they were building. This ingenious option investor flipped his deals to GM and earned over $15,000,000 (that's right, $15M) for less than 6 months of work. Maybe Mr. Onassis was right, maybe the secret to business is knowing something that no one else knows?

Pre Foreclosures

A pre foreclosure can be defined as a property that has a loan in default and is headed toward foreclosure. The length of the pre foreclosure phase can vary greatly. The state of Georgia can be as short as one month whereas New York can be six months or more. Although the pre foreclosure phase does not officially start until a foreclosure attorney sends a borrower correspondence related to their default, for our purposes, this phase can encompass any time in which a borrower is late more than 30 days on their mortgage. Most lenders have a collections process that starts when the borrower is 15 days past due on their payment.

Typically, if a borrower falls more than 90 days past due, the lender will issue a default or demand letter requesting that the entire outstanding balance be paid or the property will be foreclosed upon. Each property is different, each lender is different and certainly every state has different foreclosure laws so therefore there is no set time frame by which a property goes from past due to foreclosure. The best way to gauge the time period of a pre foreclosure is with the following two benchmarks:

Benchmark #1 – Default Letter Expiration: When a demand letter is issued, it usually contains a date by which the past-due balance must be paid. This is the expiration date of the demand/default letter. In most states, lenders must issue a demand letter with an expiration date before they can foreclose on a property.

Benchmark # 2 – Foreclosure Letter: If the borrower does not cure the past due balance and the demand letter expires, it is at this point that most lenders immediately turn the file over to an attorney. Once the file is in the attorney's hand, they usually send correspondence to the borrower starting with a letter giving the borrower an opportunity to dispute the debt. Then, right behind that initial letter you'll usually find the foreclosure letter. The foreclosure letter is a very important document. It typically outlines the time, date and location of the foreclosure auction for that property. A foreclosure letter is very serious because it marks the completion of the pre foreclosure phase and possibly the end of the borrower's ownership of the property.

Pre foreclosures can offer tremendous investing opportunities. Borrowers who are days away from a foreclosure date are typically left with very few options and can be very motivated to work out any sort of deal. This may include you paying the borrower a small amount to move out proceeded by the investor catching up the mortgage and then taking over the payments thereafter. This is also called a "subject to" and will be described in greater detail later in this section.

If there is enough equity, you can simply buy pre foreclosures outright and payoff any existing liens against the property at the closing. For pre foreclosures that are not in such a time crunch, if there is very little or no equity, you can negotiate a short sale with the foreclosing lender. Short sales will also be discussed a bit later.

For borrowers that do not want to sell their pre foreclosure property, you can even earn fees by helping homeowners negotiate loan modifications or deed in lieu of foreclosure agreements with their banks.

Some investors strictly focus on pre foreclosures and can make an absolute fortune while helping people at the same time.

Real World Example: One of our students received a call from a highly motivated seller. This property owner had purchased their home one year prior as a brand new home and had put down $40,000. The loan this borrower originated was for $100,000 and had a very low fixed interest rate making the total monthly payment a little under $800 per month. This seller has earned nearly $120,000 from a legal settlement at the time of the home purchase and had used up $40,000 for the down payment and the rest for living expenses. She went through the other $80,000 faster than she had anticipated and soon she had burned through her settlement and had no money coming in from a job. Then, she fell numerous months behind on her mortgage payments. With the foreclosure auction date only days away, she reached out to our student. This is a classic pre foreclosure deal. Our student worked out a deal whereby the seller would get $1500 cash to move out and in exchange, she would give our student the deed (transfer ownership of the property to him). Further, our student agreed to catch up the past due payments which amounted to $3500. For this seller, since she had procrastinated for so long, she really had two options. Either work with our student or get nothing and let it go to foreclosure auction. It was a no brainer for the seller because $1500 is a whole lot more than zero.

It was a no brainer for our student as well because the total out of pocket was only $5000 and he became the owner of a $140,000 property with a loan balance of a bit less than $100,000. Since the monthly payment was so low, our student leased the property to a local school teacher for $1200 and earned a monthly cash flow of nearly $400 per month. This school teacher tenant paid on time perfectly for more than 3 years providing our student with a total of nearly $15,000 in positive cash flow.

In addition to the great cash flow, the other reason why our student opted to lease the property as a long term rental was due in large part to fact that the property was in such great shape and was only one year old. Our student figured that maintenance would not be an issue since the roof, the HVAC, the hot water heater and every other component was only a year old and therefore was very unlikely to break down. Our student was right because this deal provided him with a hassle free cash flow of $400 for more than 3 years. The only work our student had to do for three years was cash the $400 cash flow check each month. How would you like an extra $400 per month, month in and month out?

It gets even better. After the tenant moved out 3 years later, our student replaced the carpet and the paint and then sold it for fair market value pocketing $35,000. This deal netted our student over $50,000 in profit from just one pre foreclosure deal.

Although investing in pre foreclosures can be quite lucrative, in recent years many laws have been enacted to protect borrowers who are in pre foreclosure. Before investing in pre foreclosures, consult a local real estate attorney who understands the details of buying pre foreclosure real estate in your area. In some states, anyone looking to purchase a home in pre foreclosure must be a licensed foreclosure consultant. In other states, a purchase contract that a distressed borrower signs to sell their property does not go into effect for a specified number of days. The idea being that a homeowner is given time to review their decision before it becomes binding. These laws were apparently put in place to protect homeowners from unscrupulous people looking to take advantage of borrowers in distress.

As stated numerous times already in this book, you should always operate legally, morally and ethically. Further, in some cases, what may be legal may not be completely moral or ethical. We suggest you go well beyond simply being legal and also operate at the highest level of moral and ethical character.

Short Sales

A short sale is an agreement from a lender to accept less than their total amount owed as payment in full for their loan. A short sale is also commonly referred to as a pre foreclosure sale because it typically occurs prior to a property being foreclosed upon by the lender (although a short sale can be done on a property that is current on payments too). A pre foreclosure deal can also be a short sale, but not always. If a borrower has plenty of equity, it can be a pre foreclosure but not require a short sale. A short sale is only needed when the loan payoff must be discounted in order to purchase the property.

Lenders typically will accept a short sale to save money over conducting a foreclosure. However, lenders do not always accept a short sale offer. The amount must be high enough to justify an approval. For example, if a lender's internal information suggests that by foreclosing they will only net 79% of the fair market value of the property, then so long as a short sale investor offers the lender more than 79%, the offer will usually be approved. On the other hand, if the investor offers 70% of fair market value, the lender may reject it. This has been the cause of so much misunderstanding and confusion surrounding short sales.

Lenders rarely accept random low ball short sale offers. They approve offers that make fiscal sense to them. If a lender thinks they will make more money by foreclosing than from accepting a low short sale offer, most lenders are not afraid to foreclose on the property. Our team has developed the Lender Database, which is the only system of its kind to provide detailed information on what lenders are approving for every major lender in the country. This allows you to be one of the rare few who know what the lender is going to agree to before you submit the offer. Without this tool, a short sale investor is operating blind. With short sales, the most important aspect is having as much knowledge about the approval process as the lender does.

> **WISDOM KEY:** You will see the term "lender" used to describe a company or a group of companies that owns and/or services mortgage loans. A loan servicing company is responsible for collecting the loan payments from borrowers. However, rarely does a loan servicing company also own the loans they service. Most mortgage loans are actually owned by institutional investors (such as pension funds, insurance companies, etc). In the lending industry, these institutional investors are referred to simply as "investors," not to be confused with what we refer to as investors, which is you. With short sales, the loan servicer handles the preparation and negotiation. However, the final approval of a short sale offer is usually determined by the investor, not the loan servicer. Since these two entities work so closely together, the term "lender" will be used to refer to both the loan servicer and the investor. In some cases, the loan servicer and the investor are one in the same as well.

It's usually quite easy to spot a short sale deal. If the borrower owes more than the value of their property, it's almost always a short sale deal. Short sales come and go with market cycles but can be found even at the height of certain up markets. The reason is that some people over leverage their properties, even in good markets, because they are short on cash. They may refinance or take out a home equity line of credit to pay bills or stay afloat financially. Since real estate costs 7% - 9% in expenses to sell (from closing costs, commissions and other fees), even properties with some equity may require a short sale in order to sell. However, short sales are most prevalent in down markets since this is when most loans go "under water" or have balances larger than the value of their underlying properties.

Some investors are attracted to short sales because they can really help a borrower from the devastating effects of a foreclosure. When all parts of a short sale deal go right, it can be a true win-win deal whereby the investor gets a great deal and the seller truly benefits as well. The challenge with short sales is that lenders are rarely efficient in their evaluation of short sale offers that are submitted to them. The negotiation process can drag on for months which can frustrate all parties involved.

Short sales have a few other benefits worthy of note. First, short sales allow you to invest in nice homes in nice areas. As opposed to HUD foreclosures (which will be discussed shortly), some short sale deals can involve multi-million dollar properties. This can be especially attractive to investors since in real estate, usually the bigger the deal, the more money you can make for doing the same amount of work as a small deal.

Second, short sales take a long time to close which gives investors who like to conduct retail wholesales plenty of time to find a retail buyer and close on the deal. Third, since the borrower is still the owner, an investor can usually sign up the deal with only $1 earnest money. And fourth, most borrowers have very little to lose since they are already upside down in their property so getting the deal under contract is usually extremely easy, even for complete real estate investing beginners.

The main drawback to short sales is the amount of time it takes to close each deal. They can range from as short as 1 month to as long as 1 year or more. The most successful short sale investors build up a pipeline of deals and then months later they begin to see their deals close one after another. Another drawback is the fact that the lender makes the ultimate decision as to whether they will agree to a short sale or not. Sometimes lenders are greedy and will not accept a deal that provides any equity. Other times lenders drag their feet and end up foreclosing prior to agreeing to a short sale. Despite these drawbacks, short sales can be extremely lucrative. Plus, in certain areas in certain market cycles, investors have no choice but to invest in short sales because sometimes it encompasses the vast majority of deals available.

> **Real World Example**: One of our students living in California during a downturn in the market was inundated with short sale leads. One of which was a homeowner who had relocated to Arizona, leaving his upside down home behind in Los Angeles. He owed nearly $780,000 on a home that was valued at only $500,000. Our student negotiated a short sale with both his first and second mortgage companies and the total short payoff was only $320,000. Our student then conducted a retail wholesale and sold the property for $460,000. After all commissions, closing costs and fees, our student walked away with nearly $90,000. This transaction did not use any cash or credit and in fact, our student could barely afford groceries days before the closing. As stated previously, when all parts of a short sale come together, it can be a tremendous win-win deal.

Foreclosures

Foreclosures are synonymous with real estate investing. Also known as an REO (which stands for Real Estate Owned), a foreclosure is a property that a bank owns and is therefore selling. Banks lend money and when their borrowers do not pay them, they legally acquire any assets that were used to collateralize their loans. In many cases, that includes real estate. The actual legal process of foreclosure is different depending on the state, but the concept in each state is the same; when borrower doesn't pay the mortgage, the bank takes the property back from the borrower.

Once the bank is the owner of the property, they usually want to sell it as quickly as possible. The first place they try to sell it is at the county courthouse, also known as a "foreclosure auction." When a bank forecloses on a property, the first thing that happens is the property is sold at auction at the local county courthouse. These auctions happen at regular intervals and in some counties, every business day.

Foreclosure Auctions

In over 90% of the cases, at the auction, no one buys the property and therefore, the bank who was owed the money becomes the highest bidder and ends up with the property. The other 10% that are purchased typically occur from experienced investors. Buying real estate at foreclosure auctions typically requires immediate cash to fund the purchase. In fact, in many counties, the money must be in the hands of the attorney handling the foreclosure in as short as 1 hour. That means that the money must be ready and available prior to the auction. This makes it very difficult to finance through most funding channels and only those investors with cash in the bank usually can buy these deals. Plus, due to the very tight time constraints, some foreclosure auction buyers must work in teams whereby one person is at the bank ready to create the cashier's check while the other is at the actual auction bidding on the property, in order to actually buy the property. Thankfully for foreclosure auction buyers, a new trend is immerging whereby foreclosure auctions are now being held online. If the county closest to you has not moved their foreclosure auction process completely online, hopefully it will sometime soon.

Unless an investor has an inside track on a deal, most foreclosure auctions involve the purchasing of "sight unseen" real estate. In which case, the investor has not been able to conduct an inspection and is therefore unaware of all the issues that may be plaguing the property. The ability to conduct a thorough inspection is really important when buying any type of property. Further, there are so many other ways to buy real estate that putting yourself in a situation where you are being forced to buy something sight unseen may not be the best way to go about investing.

Another important detail not to overlook when buying real estate at foreclosure auctions is that some liens can actually reside against the property after the foreclosure (even though it is commonly thought that a foreclosure wipes out all liens). Therefore, an investor may not be able to obtain clear title to the property for a period of time after the sale. IRS tax liens oftentimes survive foreclosure for a period of six months. In some states, owners are given a right of redemption period by law and it allows the previous owner up to 6 months (even a year in some cases) to buy back the property.

If you are going to be buying properties at the foreclosure auction in redemption states, you will need to find out exactly how the right of redemption process works. If there is anyway another person can buy property after a foreclosure auction, it is imperative that you as the investor know how long until you are in the clear. It would be quite devastating to put in time and effort to improve a property only to discover that the previous homeowner is going to purchase the home back through a right of redemption.

One last item to consider when buying property at foreclosure auction is that the previous owner may still be living in the home so you may have to evict them to get full possession of the property. If you have never gone through the eviction process before, it would be wise to learn how eviction works in your county before buying real estate at a foreclosure auction.

> **WISDOM KEY:** You will find that in real estate, it is both state and county specific. Each state has its own set of laws governing real estate. A few common examples would be right of redemption states and attorney closing states. Further, each county handles certain aspects of real estate differently as well. The most common example of this is the way in which eviction is handled. Each county law within your state could be markedly different as it pertains to eviction law. As a rule of thumb, fast cash techniques are usually state specific and long term wealth building techniques are usually county specific.

As you can see, there are many challenges facing foreclosure auction investors. Still, great buying opportunities do exist and there are ways to reduce some of the risks. Most notably, if you have already conducted a detailed inspection of the property prior to the auction, reviewed the title, obtained a redemption waiver from the owner (if in a redemption state) and have the money lined up ahead of time, even a relative novice can responsibly attempt a foreclosure auction purchase. And since there are so many "barriers to entry" with this strategy, there are usually only a few people in any given county that attempt to buy at foreclosure auctions and therefore, with less competition, comes the prospects of getting more great deals.

> **Real World Example:** For one of our students, this particular deal was not going her way, or so she thought. Since the property owner had contacted her so late in the pre foreclosure phase, there was very little time to negotiate a short sale with the lender. Before she could obtain the final approval, the property went to foreclosure auction. She knew the property well, conservatively estimating that its value was $130,000 as a residential property but since it was also zoned commercial, it had the potential to be worth $200,000 or more as a professional office building. Her negotiations with the bank during the pre foreclosure short sale phase indicated to her that the lender would not take less than $100,000. She decided to attend the foreclosure auction just to see what would happen. Our student arrived completely unprepared to make a bid on the property because she made the mistake of assuming that the bank would open the bidding at the same level she had been negotiating at during the short sale period. To her surprise, the opening bid was much lower than $100,000. It started at $70,000! She watched in disgust as another investor snatched up the deal for $70,001.

And this investor had based his numbers on what the property would bring as a residential property.

Much to his delight, when he discovered it could be rented to a dentist, or attorney or other business, his $70,000 investment became a $200,000 commercial property that brought $2,000 per month in rent. As you can see, in certain situations, the foreclosure auction can present incredible opportunities, especially when you have followed the property through the pre foreclosure process and have inspected the property. The lesson to also gain from this example is to never assume what the lender is going to open the bid for at a foreclosure auction. You may just be pleasantly surprised.

Pre-List Foreclosures

The next phase after a bank acquires a property through a foreclosure auction is called the "Pre-List" stage (the phrase was coined because it is the time before the property is listed on the MLS). In this stage, the bank owns the property and is in the process of preparing it for market.

They usually have to perform the following actions: First, they assign the property to a real estate agent (referred to as an REO agent). Second, they usually hire an appraiser to assess the value of the property. Third, the REO agent typically gets the property cleaned out, removing the junk and debris and possibly even replacing the carpet or adding a fresh coat of paint.

In some cases, the previous owners may still be living in the home and the bank may have to evict them. Usually the bank starts with a "friendly eviction" where they pay the squatters $500 to move out of the property and keep it in good condition on the way out. If that doesn't work, they progress to hiring an attorney, filing the eviction paperwork and eventually having a sheriff physically remove them from the property.

During this "Pre-List" phase, it has been the desire of many real estate investors to negotiate with the bank and attempt to buy the property before the bank has to go through all the pre-list hassles. Although this does exist in some rare cases, the vast majority of banks are smart enough to know that getting the property listed on the MLS is the best way to get the highest priced offer for their property. Getting a property on the MLS is a very powerful marketing plan and is usually the best way to get the highest priced buyer.

Other creative investors have attempted to work with the agent who was assigned to the property and attempt to work out a side deal. The problem with this strategy is that banks once again, aren't stupid, they know this trick, and in most cases, require the REO agent to keep the property on the MLS for a minimum number of days to allow as many offers to come in as possible. Further, asking a real estate agent to work a side deal could be unethical and could put the agent's license in jeopardy. Again, always operate legally, ethically and in such a manner that you can be proud of if it was plastered on the front page of a newspaper.

There are a few hidden ways to put together a pre list foreclosure deal. The first way is with a local or small bank that isn't well versed in how to most effectively market and dispose of their foreclosure properties. With some small, local banks, their REO asset manager may wear numerous hats in the organization and may be willing to work directly with an investor if they feel it will bring less hassles than handing over the listing to an agent. If the bank is nationwide, large and well established, it will usually be quite difficult to attempt to buck their well entrenched system and try to buy the property in the pre-list stage.

The second way to find a pre list foreclosure is through top producing REO agents that are hired by large institutional investors or hedge funds to sell off their portfolios of distressed assets. Large banks that handle thousands of foreclosures each year sometimes have issues selling a small percentage of their properties. One quick solution to selling all of these misfits quickly is to bundle them up and sell them as a package deal. The buyers of these bulk REO packages tend to be distressed asset private equity funds and hedge funds. Once the owner of these bulk REO packages, they usually hire the best local REO agents to sell the properties they just bought. Since these properties are not under the same stringent foreclosure guidelines as banks, some REO agents have the flexibility to sell these types of deals pre list. Bulk REO deals do not come along very often so these deals are few and far between. But, when they do come along, you can oftentimes get a really good deal.

The third way to find a pre list deal is applicable in states that have a right of redemption period. A right of redemption is an extraordinary loophole that very few investors know anything about but can be incredibly powerful. A right of redemption gives a homeowner the right to buy back the property after the foreclosure auction. This right of redemption can also be transferred or sold to a third party such as an investor. As opposed to buying properties at the foreclosure auction, if investing in a right of redemption state, you can actually focus on connecting with the homeowners, purchasing their right of redemption and then purchasing the property prior to the redemption period expiration. As it stands right now, the following list shows

the states that have a right of redemption period for home-
owners as well as the length of time it lasts:
  • Alabama: 1 year
  • Iowa: 60 days to 6 months
  • Kansas: 1 year
  • Kentucky: 1 year
  • Maine: 90 days
  • Michigan: 6 months (1 year for 5+ acre properties)
  • Minnesota: 6 months
  • New Jersey: 10 days
  • New Mexico: 9 months
  • North Dakota: 60 days (1 yr for agricultural)
  • Oregon: 6 months
  • South Dakota: 1 year (60 days for vacant properties)
  • Vermont: 6 months (1 year for properties built pre-1968)
  • Wisconsin: 1 year
  • Wyoming: 3 months
    This list is not complete as there are numerous states
that have a right of redemption provision in their foreclosure
laws. However, many of these also allow lenders to place in
the original loan paperwork a waiver of redemption rights.
The details of this subject can actually become quite complex
so the states listed above are considered to be the easiest and
most straight right of redemption states. In addition, even
the list above has numerous caveats so before attempting a
right of redemption deal in your state, consult a foreclosure
attorney well versed in this subject.
    A right of redemption deal has numerous benefits.
First, very few other investors know these provisions exist
and therefore you typically have very little competition.
Second, the property is not listed on the MLS during this
time so you can re-sell the property on the most powerful
marketing tool in real estate (the MLS). Third, since you

already know what the property went to foreclosure auction for, you know the bank's bottom line and therefore the negotiation is usually much easier. Fourth, after the foreclosure auction, attention to the property from other investors usually subsides so there is typically no one else reaching out to these deals. Fifth, the bank is unable to sell or market the property during the redemption period so in many cases, it sits vacant, a silent opportunity just waiting for you to pick up.

The main drawback is that only a select few states have laws enacted making it advantageous for investors to focus their attention on right of redemption deals. Further, obtaining a property through right of redemption is a little different than usual and since each state is different, you will need to connect with an attorney who knows exactly how the right of redemption purchasing process works.

Real World Example: Rather than contact sellers in pre foreclosure, one student in a right of redemption state chose to target the owners whose properties had just been foreclosed upon at the foreclosure auction. He would obtain the list from the local county recorder and scour the list for those properties that had a foreclosure auction price of far lower than the fair market value. About 5% of the list would have promising prospects. He would then reach out to this select few through phone, mail and even a personal visit to the property to ask the neighbors how to reach the owner. One particular owner he contacted was more than willing to sell his right of redemption to our student in exchange for buying the property prior to the redemption expiration because it would reverse the foreclosure on his credit report. The bank agreed to the same amount as their opening auction bid and as soon as our student obtained the approval, he immediately put it on the MLS. Within a few weeks, he had a full price offer. It closed about 30 days later and our student pocketed more than $33,000. He used no cash and no credit. He simply retail wholesaled a right of redemption deal. This student does these deals over and over because they are so straight forward and lucrative.

Bank Owned REO Auctions

There exists another small segment of the foreclosure population that is not listed on the MLS and this includes REO auctions. Sometimes local banks want to get rid of their foreclosures so quickly that they skip the step of assigning it to a REO agent and immediately hire a local auction company to auction it off. These are usually absolute auctions, meaning the highest bidder gets the deal, regardless of how high that bid is. Therefore, if only one person shows up to the auction, it could be the greatest deal ever. That normally doesn't happen though because the auctioneer's job is to ensure as many buyers show up to the auction as possible.

One bonus that this type of auction has over the foreclosure auction is that the auction company can usually arrange financing for the buyer provided they can put 10% to 20% down or the buyer can use their own financing source and the buyer usually has up to 30 days to close. These types of auctions are much easier to purchase from a financing standpoint, they usually offer clear title (although never assume this) and they usually allow prospective buyers to inspect the property prior to the bidding. For these reasons, the typical REO auction is a whole lot easier to buy a property at than the foreclosure auction. But this also means you may have more competition.

There are also a few types of rare government foreclosures that are auctioned off, including those properties that have been seized by the IRS or through a criminal being arrested and all of their possessions being seized by the government. In these cases, the government usually hires an auction company to sell the property to the highest bidder. The easiest way to learn about these deals is to visit the various websites that post this information.

Listed Foreclosures

Thus far, we have covered the instances where a foreclosure or REO is sold through a means other than the MLS. That class encompasses the small minority of foreclosures. The vast majority end up listed on the MLS with an REO agent. Why? As stated earlier, listing a property on the MLS is a very powerful marketing strategy and usually nets the highest sales price for a property. The problem with a listed foreclosure is that once it hits the MLS, everyone else knows about the deal and this creates competition. Rockefeller was quoted as having said, "Competition is a sin."

As the number of competitors increase, you're chances of getting a great deal decrease. Plus, when a property goes on the MLS, you are now in direct competition with retail buyers, those buyers that want to live in the property and they are almost always willing to pay far more than an investor for a property.

You may be asking, "How can I find good deals among listed foreclosures?" There are a few inconsistencies in this otherwise completely efficient marketing style that you can focus on. First, if the property is in complete disrepair, it may intimidate a retail buyer and therefore you are left with only other investor buyers for the property. Next, if a foreclosure listing sits on the market for a long time at a price too high for any investor to buy it, it can go unnoticed over time. After an extended number of days on the market, usually 120 days, most banks open their minds to lower offers so you can slip in with an offer far lower than the list price. As long as it has been on the market for a very long time, you may have a chance at getting a surprisingly good deal.

A fabulous inconsistency in the listed foreclosure world occurs when banks must liquidate large chunks of foreclosures for financial purposes. Oftentimes, they will package up blocks of foreclosures that have been sitting on the market for several months and sell them in a bulk package. Right before the property gets wrapped up in a bulk package, the asset manager and the REO agent will both quickly scramble for a buyer, even if they must discount the property dramatically, because if the property gets put into a bulk package, neither the REO agent or the asset manager benefit. They become desperate and that creates a great opportunity for you!

How do you take advantage of these inconsistencies? Network with the top producing REO agents in your area. These types of real estate agents may close anywhere from 50 to 500 or more transactions per year. They run a very productive real estate operation and therefore do not have a whole lot of extra time on their hands. In order to get noticed by these super star REO agents, you must be able to close quickly with cash. This ability to move fast on a great deal requires several skills that you may need to develop overtime. When you start trying to do deals with top producing REO agents, you are truly, "playing with the big boys," and need to have your ducks in a row.

Some beginner investors have complained, "There aren't any foreclosure deals out there because my real estate agent says that as soon as any foreclosure hits the market, there are instantly multiple offers from cash buyers." This scenario may be true in certain areas during certain market cycles. That's why banks prefer to market their foreclosures on the MLS, it works! However, in any market, there are usually at least a few deals that get overlooked, usually under the circumstances described above. As a successful person, you shouldn't be worried about all the reasons why something won't work. Instead, you should be focused on all the ways something will work.

> **WISDOM KEY:** Many listed foreclosures have a requirement that can be quite frustrating to investors. The listing agent will require that anyone looking to make an offer on the property pre-qualify with the bank who owns the property. Not that you have to use that financing source, but that you must qualify through them in order to be able to even submit an offer. This alone kicks out many investors from being able to make an offer. As you can see, banks want retail buyers purchasing their foreclosures (as do we when we are selling our own deals).

HUD Foreclosures

When a loan is backed by FHA (Federal Housing Administration) and the borrower stops paying the note, the property is foreclosed upon and ends up in the hands of HUD (Housing and Urban Development). Also referred to as "HUD Homes", investors are usually prevented from purchasing these foreclosures in the first 30 or so days it is listed. The government uses these homes to help certain groups of people achieve homeownership. For example, in many areas, policemen, firemen and school teachers are given down payment assistance or other incentives to purchase HUD homes. They can be a great deal for someone in the public service sector.

> **WISDOM KEY:** If you're a policeman, fireman or school teacher, do some research to find out if your area provides incentives if you buy a HUD home. It could be the best deal going out there for you. You may be able to pick up a great home for as little as 50% of value.

Also, during states of emergency, HUD homes can be used to house emergency evacuees. After Katrina, all HUD homes in the Southeast were pulled off the market and given to Louisiana evacuees for temporary housing.

This begs the question, "When are HUD homes a potentially good investment?" After the initial period whereby only owner occupied buyers can make an offer, this is where investors can begin to make offers. Although some opportunities may exist among HUD homes that have just been released from the owner occupied period, in most cases, the best HUD home deals begin after the property has been on the market for a minimum of 120 days. Some investors simply submit low ball offers to every listed HUD home on the 121st day it is on the market. Very few HUD homes ever make it that far, but when they do, HUD is far easier to negotiate with and some opportunities do exist.

> **WISDOM KEY:** When it comes to investing in foreclosures, you're almost always dealing strictly with

price. Although more common in the past, these days, most banks rarely offer buyers of foreclosures good terms unless the buyer has great credit, tons of easily verifiable income and a very large down payment (or the buyer is going to live in the home as in the case of HUD foreclosures or VA foreclosures). In most cases, as an investor, you're dealing with really only one variable; price. This is also known as a straight line negotiation because the lower the price you negotiate, the better the deal. Also, you are rarely given more than about 30 days to close so wholesaling a foreclosure requires that you already have buyers on speed dial and can find and get a new buyer ready to close in less than 30 days.

Real World Example: A very successful investor who owns nearly 150 single family homes has built his mini-empire from the following formula: As a licensed real estate agent, he set up an auto-reminder that alerted him every time a HUD foreclosure listing went 120 days on the market. Every so often, he would get an alert and he would immediately submit a low ball offer on the property. Over time, a certain percentage of these offers he submitted got accepted. He used local banks to finance the purchases of these properties since he had both cash and credit. After improving each property, instead of immediately re-selling them, he would sell them on a rent to own. Since less than 20% of tenant buyers exercise their option to purchase, over a long period of time, his portfolio grew to nearly 150 houses and each one has tremendous equity and cash flow.His formula has three major advantages. First, he was buying these properties at a very low price so he has tons of equity. If the tenant doesn't pay him and he is forced to evict, if he is tight on cash, he can always sell the property quickly because he has so much room in the deal. Second, since he buys them so cheap and he uses a local bank loan, he has low monthly payments so he can cash flow strong. Third, since he sells them after owning the property for more than a year, he gets the tax benefit of paying long term capital gains tax as opposed to ordinary income tax on the profit.

VA Foreclosures

When a VA loan goes unpaid and is foreclosed upon, the Veteran Affairs Administration will list the property with an REO agent just like almost every other foreclosure. However, they also offer favorable financing terms so that the property is within reach of almost anyone. For investors, the requirements can be as low as 5% down and there is no limit to the number of "VA Vendee Loans" that an investor can have. Plus (and this may be the best part of all), the investor can use up to 75% of the anticipated rents as income on the loan application. Very few, if any, conventional loan programs allow borrowers to claim income on a rental property that is not yet rented. In most cases, you must already have the tenant moved into the property with a signed lease in order to use the rental income as part of your income on a loan application. The terms of a VA vendee loan are very good, making this a little known niche within the foreclosure realm potentially extremely profitable.

There are a few minor drawbacks though. First, the property is listed so there will be some competition. Second, there aren't very many of these deals out there. The VA posts every active VA foreclosure on their website. When you search for VA foreclosures in your entire state, you may be surprised by how few there are. Third, because the terms are so amazing, the price you pay may be a bit higher than with an all cash auction type deal.

The investors who stand to profit the most from this niche are those that live near a military base where VA loans are used most frequently. These areas will create the most VA foreclosures and also, will provide a steady stream of potential tenants in the event the investor wants to buy and hold the VA foreclosures they purchase.

Tax Lien Certificates & Deeds

A special type of local government seizure involves the selling of a tax lien certificate and the conducting of a tax deed sale. With a tax lien certificate sale, the local property taxes go past due and the way the county collects the money is to offer local investors a guaranteed interest rate if they will pay the delinquent tax property owner's bill. In other words, if you buy a tax lien certificate, you are actually paying someone else's property tax bill for them in exchange for guaranteed interest on your money or the prospect of becoming the owner of the property. If the property owner doesn't pay you back plus interest, you then have the ability to become the owner of the property, sometimes for pennies on the dollar.

For example, if the county is owed $10,000 in property taxes, you would pay $10,000 for the tax lien certificate. The property owner would then have a period of time, in some cases 1 year, to payback the entire amount plus interest (which can range from as low as 3% to as much as 25%+). If the property owner does not payback the $10,000 amount plus the interest, the tax lien certificate holder may have the ability to foreclose on the property and become the owner.

This is where you may have heard stories of real estate investors paying 10 cents on the dollar for real estate. It does happen. The best part about tax sales is that the money invested will, in most cases, come back to you plus interest. In fact, many institutional investors understand the value of such remarkable returns with such little risk and have begun showing up at tax sale auctions as well. Don't be surprised if the person sitting next to you at your next local tax lien certificate auction is a bank representative looking to buy investments.

While that may sound like a dream come true to pick up a property for 10 cents on the dollar, or at the very least to generate guaranteed returns on your investment, there are a few pitfalls to tax lien certificate investing. The first challenge is that you need real cash that you can allow to stay tied up for a minimum of one year. Although you can borrow the money from a private money source, it is usually far better to use your own cash and for many investors, they simply do not have access to that kind of extra cash that can be tied up for over a year. Second, in some states, you have to buy the tax lien certificate on the property every year for several years to maintain the first position to foreclose. Therefore, you will need to have money available in the future to continue to keep buying more tax lien certificates. Third, it can oftentimes be difficult to obtain title insurance on tax lien certificate properties that you foreclose on. That means that you may be unable to sell the property to someone else since you are unable to furnish a title insurance policy yourself.

Fourth, the property may be in a state that has homestead rights which may allow the homeowner to continue to reside in the property for years before you can remove them. As the owner, you may have to maintain the property to keep the city or county codes department happy, including mowing and otherwise maintaining the property to minimum codes standards. If a person is occupying the property, that still means you have to keep the property up to codes standards, which can be altogether frustrating, mowing the lawn of a property you don't collect rent on.

Fifth, you may acquire a property that is completely locked with no access points or easements. This is very common when a large tract of land is split up over time and then eventually all that is left is one sliver of land that has no easements or access points and simply sits surrounded by other people's land. It can be very difficult to sell or lease that type of property unless one of the neighbors will buy or rent it. That is sometimes the reason why a property goes to tax sale. The owner doesn't want it anymore and it is actually worth to the owner just to let the county take it off their hands so that they don't have to deal with the yearly property taxes, the maintenance or the headaches anymore.

> **WISDOM KEY:** The best tax sale deals involve an owner who simply procrastinates to the point where it is too late. An example would be a property one of our students dealt with that was worth $60,000 and was rented for $600 per month through Section 8. It was owned outright but the owner was so busy dealing with other issues that he forgot to pay the property taxes and then later, puts off the letters about the tax lien, then still later procrastinated the deadline to pay back the tax lien plus interest. And before he knew it, the tax lien had matured and the tax lien owner was going to foreclose to gain ownership from buying a $2000 tax lien certificate.

The way a tax lien investor becomes the owner of the property is through a foreclosure. If the homeowner does not payback the tax lien plus the interest, the tax lien investor can foreclose to gain ownership. It is through this process that some title insurers refuse to issue title insurance. That is why it is critically important that before you invest in any tax lien certificate, you find out if other tax lien investors in the county in which you will be investing in are obtaining title insurance. If the homeowner does payback the tax lien, the benefit to the investor is the interest on their money.

In some areas, the city handles the foreclosure process and you can purchase the property at a tax deed auction. With a tax deed sale, the property owner fails to pay back the outstanding tax liens and then the county auctions off the property to the highest bidder. Tax deed auctions are similar to any other auctions and the key is to know the property before buying.

The beauty and challenge of tax lien & deed investing is that it is very state and county specific. In some areas of the country, it can be extremely profitable, but in others, it can be a minefield of traps and problems. Further, some of the best areas are saddled with competition because most state and county tax lien & deed rules and guidelines are public information. It is very easy to get access to the details so anyone who has a couple bucks becomes a competitor. And as you have already discovered, the more competition there is, the more difficult it is to get a great deal.

Tax lien and deed investing is also very property specific. Single family homes usually a mortgage on the property and right before an auction, the mortgage company will usually pay the money to cover the property taxes so that they don't get wiped out (property taxes supersede all other liens). Some institutional investors actually far prefer this outcome and therefore purposefully only buy tax lien certificates on properties that have a large first mortgage so that they can be assured they get their interest. On the other hand, most real estate investors would far prefer the prospects of getting a property for pennies on the dollar. They focus on the properties that are not likely to redeem (have the tax lien paid back) which are typically those without a loan. Then, there are the pitfalls of buying bad properties.

The key to successfully investing in tax liens and deeds is to understand the rules and regulations for the specific county and to know each property that you are bidding on. For most successful tax sale investors, a combination of experience and homework are required.

Creative Financing

Up to this point, you have learned about many of the traditional ways to buy real estate; wholesaling, pre foreclosures, short sales and the vast subject of foreclosures. Now, you're going to learn about purchasing or controlling real estate using creative financing. These strategies are far less known but can be extremely powerful. Since so few people are aware of these different ways of buying or controlling real estate, you will have less competition when you apply them. Plus, they have many hidden benefits that most of the traditional investing strategies do not. But, this section also requires that you step outside the normal real estate box. These are creative approaches.

Subject To

The phrase "subject to" is actually a shortened version of the phrase, "subject to the existing financing." Believe it or not, you can be the owner of a property without your name ever appearing on the loan. If you were to buy a property whereby the existing loans did not get paid off, you would be buying the property "subject to the existing financing."

This scenario happens more often than you might think. For example, if a couple gets married and prior to the marriage, one spouse owned a home and the other one didn't, in many states, as soon as the two are married, both become equal owners of the home. Therefore, one spouse becomes part owner even though he or she is not on the loan. This person therefore owns the property, "subject to the existing financing." The reason why this is possible is because the owner of the property is signified by a deed while a mortgage is secured against a property with a completely separate recorded instrument. Therefore, you can have a homeowner execute a deed giving you ownership of their property while leaving the current loan in place and making no changes to the loan documentation.

For many investors, a "subject to" deal is a dream come true. First, it allows you to become the owner of real estate without cash or credit. Second, oftentimes an owner occupied loan (which is what most sellers have in place on their property) have far better loan terms than the non-owner occupied loans that investors get. Third, many single family homes can only cash flow positive if a very low fixed interest rate loan is in place on the property so the "subject to" approach provides a way to open up a whole new class of properties to long term investors. Fourth, it allows investors to purchase unlimited numbers of properties, something that conventional lenders cap investors on. And fifth, many investors like the idea that they can own real estate without their name on the loan. That way, if things go south financially for them, their credit is not affected.

> **WISDOM KEY:** As a responsible, moral and ethical investor, you should always treat a subject to deal as if your name was on the loan. If you buy a property subject to the existing financing, the seller in good faith is counting on you to fulfill your obligation to make the monthly payments on time. Therefore, choose your subject to purchases wisely so that you always can fulfill your promises.

The "subject to" technique works for both fast cash and long term wealth building pursuits. As opposed to purchasing the traditional way and then improving it, some investors simply buy the property subject to the existing financing and then come out of pocket the money to improve it and then they sell it to a retail buyer. Other investors use the subject to as a way to build a large portfolio of rental properties. You can purchase virtually unlimited properties in this fashion.

The key to the subject to is whether or not the seller is motivated enough to allow you to become the owner while keeping the loan in their name. To the inexperienced, it may at first appear insane to think anyone would agree to sell their property and keep their name on the loan. But, when you get out there and start talking to motivated seller, you will find that some sellers will beg you to take their property off their hands.

In fact, in certain circumstances, a "subject to" can actually be a borrower's best option. This occurs when a borrower falls behind on mortgage payments. If that borrower does not catch up the late payments but instead either lets the property go to foreclosure or sells the property and pays off the loan while in default, it can really damage their credit rating. However, if the payments are caught up and then are kept up to date for a period of time, (which is what happens when an investor buys a property subject to, they will catch up any outstanding payments and then pay mortgage payments moving forward on time), the borrower's credit rating can be vastly improved. For sellers that do not have access to the money to catch up the payments, having an investor bring the loan current can be the very best outcome for that seller.

Subject to investing has always been somewhat controversial. The main controversy centers around a certain clause most mortgage companies put in their loan documentation called a "due on sale" clause. This clause usually goes something along the lines of, "if the property changes ownership, the lender reserves the right to call the loan due." When a lender calls a loan due, they expect their entire loan balance within a very short period of time or else they will begin the foreclosure process. In the annals of real estate investing history, there have been very few (less than 0.001%) incidences of a lender calling a loan due from a transfer of title of a subject to transaction. The factors that have led to these occurrences have usually been that the loan was not current, had fallen into default and the lender saw an opportunity to initiate foreclosure faster than the normal way by using the violation of the due on sale clause.

The reason why so few lenders enforce the "due on sale" clause is because banks are in the business of lending and collecting money and in most cases, they want to continue to own and service a performing asset (a loan that is being paid on time) as opposed to acquiring it through foreclosure. As a subject to investor, continuing to make on time payments is critical to ensuring you bring no unneeded attention to your deal. If the payments are made on time, most lenders (99.999%) will never bother with enforcing the due on sale clause.

Finally, even if a lender was to call the loan due, so long as you had purchased the property right, you could sell it or refinance it well within the time the lender specified to be fully paid. If you are making payments on time to the mortgage company, your odds of experiencing a lender accelerate a loan due to a title change is far less than being struck by lightning. In other words, for most subject to investors, the thought of a lender foreclosing as a result of the "due on sale" clause never crosses their mind.

> **WISDOM KEY:** Some investors have circumvented the due on sale clause by deeding the property into a trust that the homeowner has a partial beneficial

interest in. This satisfies the stipulations in most due on sale clauses because the borrower maintains an ownership position in the property. The problem with this arrangement is that the original owner is still involved in the transaction and history will prove that when you keep the owner involved, trouble usually ensues. You are welcome to try out this method but records show that as clever as this may at first appear, in practice, it's far better to make it a clean transaction by not leaving the previous seller as a part owner. Since the odds of a loan being called due is so small, taking on this additional liability and risk with keeping the original owner involved simply doesn't make sense for most investors.

Lease Purchase

The lease purchase is a technique that shares many of the same characteristics as the "subject to". With a lease purchase, the investor is leasing the property from the owner and is also securing an option to purchase the property for a specified period of time.

By entering into this arrangement, you are controlling the property as opposed to owning it, which can have numerous benefits. First, if your name is not on the property, it doesn't show up in any records that you are the owner which may provide anonymity in the event you accumulate a colossal portfolio of real estate holdings and want to remain under the radar. Second, if the deal does not pan out, so long as your lease purchase agreement is written correctly, you may be able to give the property back quickly and easily without the headaches that sometimes occur with giving back a subject to deal. Third, since you are not the owner, technically there isn't a closing which saves you money when you acquire the property. And fourth, leases can sometimes be extremely powerful and allow you to control the property without the responsibilities of ownership.

Real World Example: Most people are familiar with the iconic building in downtown New York City, the Empire State Building. What most passers by would probably be blissfully unaware of is the fact that the Empire State Building has been controlled by a bulletproof long term lease for a very long time and will continue to be for many years to come. The building, if not locked in by this lease, could be worth $1B or more. As it stands right now, its value is a fraction of that amount. The reason is that the long term lease that is in place has a rental rate that is much, much lower than the market rental rate. Commercial real estate is often valued by the amount of income it produces. The Empire State Building produces a fraction of the amount of income it could produce had this lease not be in place.

Many ambitious real estate tycoons, including Donald Trump, have attempted to break the lease in the past but each time it has been brought into the local courts, the lease has held strong. Nearly 28 high powered attorneys long ago crafted this work of art and it has made the beneficiaries of this deal an absolute fortune.

The principals that control the lease actually re-lease the individual office space to other tenants. This is referred to as a "sandwich lease". When an investor controls a property through a lease and then re-leases the property to a tenant, they are conducting a "sandwich lease" arrangement. This is not allowed in all states so make sure you verify with a local real estate attorney before embarking on a sandwich lease deal. For the Empire State Building lessors, the cash flow they receive by simply controlling the building through their lease is extraordinary. In fact, over time, these principals have passed on their rights to their heirs making this a dynasty.

The one item the Empire State Building lease is missing is the option to purchase the property. In fact, ownership of the Empire State Building has changed hands numerous times over the years and throughout all of these changes, the lease remains in force. As an investor working with motivated sellers, they are often very interested in the property being sold sometime in the near future so that they can fully wipe their hands clean of the property. Therefore, in most cases, you will not only be controlling the property through a lease, you will also have the option to purchase the property.

The biggest drawback to acquiring a property on a lease purchase arrangement is that the owner still has his/her name on the title and therefore, if that person has a lien or judgment slapped against him/her, that debt could end up filed against your deal. That could then wipe out any future profits when you try to sell it. There are some ways to protect yourself somewhat from this potential catastrophe, but the only surefire way to insulate yourself from such an occurrence is to buy the property through a subject to arrangement.

WISDOM KEY: As a general rule, if the deal is good enough, if you are going to be re-selling the property to a rent to own tenant buyer, it is usually best to

purchase the property subject to and to only drop
down to the lease purchase level if the seller won't
agree to a subject to arrangement.

Owner Financing

Another way to acquire real estate creatively is to have
the owner of the property provide the financing for you. This
can take on many forms but the basic concept is that instead
of you bringing money to the transaction, you agree to pay
the owner back overtime. In situations where the property is
owned free and clear (without a loan), the subject to strategy
is not applicable and if you want to own the property as
opposed to control it with a lease purchase, you either have
to bring your own money to the closing or you have to get the
seller to finance the purchase for you.

There are many benefits to acquiring property with
owner financing. First, most owners will not check your
credit or verify your income as in the case of borrowing
money from a bank. Second, the terms of the loan can sometimes be far more favorable than a bank. Third, most property owners do not have the wherewithal to report payments
to the credit bureaus so the loan may not appear on your
credit report. And fourth, it may be the only way for you to
acquire a property that is owned free and clear.

There are benefits to the seller as well. Some property
owners may not have a loan against their real estate and
might be in the process of retiring. In such cases, a big chunk
of cash may not be nearly as important to this seller as a
steady monthly stream of income. Many sellers can avoid the
gigantic tax bill that may be triggered from the sale of the
property by selling it on an "installment sale". An installment
sale is a type of owner financing whereby the deed is not

transferred to the new buyer until the entire purchase amount is paid off. It can be accomplished whereby the seller only pays tax on the income that is generated per year from the monthly payments. This can be highly advantageous to certain sellers.

Although buying a property through owner financing may provide you with very favorable loan terms, as a seller you may want to think twice before offering to sell a property to someone else whereby you are the one providing the owner financing. The reason is that by selling one of your own properties on owner financing terms, you will have to use the legal foreclosure process in order to take back possession of the property if the person stops paying you. Foreclosure can take months and months to complete and can be very costly.

Large lending institutions can weather the storm of a foreclosure much easier than you can because they are not lending their own money in most cases. The way our banking system works is that banks lend approximately 10 times the amount that they have in deposits. They lend 10 times more money than they have and there isn't a vault somewhere that houses that extra money either. They are lending money out of thin air! If you were lending money out of thin air, waiting six months to a year before you acquired your property back would not be as devastating but since you would be owner financing real money, foreclosure is a very expensive proposition.

WISDOM KEY: To learn more about how the banking system works, there are numerous books, publications and resources that describe this fascinating (and infuriating once you know the truth) subject. The book "The Creature from Jekyll Island" by Edward

---

Griffin is the definitive text on the topic although it is very long. You may also find terrific resources online by searching the phrase, "The Truth behind Our Banking System". Caution though, once you go down this rabbit hole, you may never see the world quite the same again. It's really sad when you find out that the money banks lend is largely created out of thin air.

When selling a property, it is almost always much better to maintain ownership and control of the property by offering to the buyer a rent to own arrangement. That way, if the person stops paying you, you wouldn't be foreclosing, but instead, you would be evicting the person as a tenant. Evictions can be very fast depending on the county in which your property is located, but usually they take less than 30 days if you hire the right eviction attorney.

There is a bit of a double standard being presented here. As a buyer of real estate, the owner financing strategy can be a terrific tool in your investor tool belt, but as a seller of real estate, it is usually much safer to avoid owner financing and to use the rent to own arrangement. Like all real estate deals, each situation is different and there may be times where selling using owner financing is advantageous. One example would be where a buyer only needs you as the seller to "carry back" or owner finance 10% of the purchase price. This happens in situations where the buyer is short the down payment but can obtain a loan for say, 90% of the purchase.

Real World Example: One of our students had renovated a property in a working class part of town and one particular buyer was willing to pay more than full price for the property but her mortgage company could only provide 90% of the total sales price. This buyer did not have the other 10% in a bank account, she couldn't get a relative to help her and she couldn't find another bank to lend her the additional amount. Our student reasoned that if the property would appraise for more than his asking price, he could reasonably raise the purchase price to a level whereby taking back a note for that 10% would not cut too deeply into his profits. As it turned out, the appraiser came back with an amount higher than his asking price so he was able to raise the price to the level of the appraisal amount. Instead of bringing that 10% money to the closing table, since our student was the owner, he owner financed that 10% by having the closing company draft a mortgage note for the amount. This buyer was very motivated to purchase the home so our student was able to charge an interest rate that would provide a small additional profit as well.

When the deal closed, the buyer's first mortgage wired 90% of the purchase to the closing company. This was just about the same amount as his original asking price. The other 10% came as an owner finance note from our student. This provided our student with a steady monthly check from the buyer and to our student, was basically an extra bonus on top of what he had already profited. His attitude was that if the borrower didn't ever pay him, he still made out just fine. The only problem with this otherwise brilliant plan was that from a tax perspective, our student had to pay income taxes on the 10% note as well even though he had not received that money in his hand in that calendar year. The way he planned to off set this predicament was that he would have the buyer make on time payments for 6 months and then he could sell this "seasoned" and "performing" note to a note buyer. Then, if he was able to sell his note within that same calendar year, even though he would have to pay income taxes on the 10% amount, at least he would have some cash from the sale of the note to cover the taxes and also have a healthy amount left over.

All was going according to plan until the buyer filed Chapter 13 bankruptcy just 5 months after buying the home. The bankruptcy court sent a few more payments sporadically and then the payments stopped coming in altogether. In the end, the note was not sold to note buyer because it became a "non performing note". All was not lost however because our student used the 7 or so payments to off set the tax liability. The lesson here is to never assume that someone is going to pay you on your owner financed note and therefore, only do it if it is icing on the cake and you have already obtained your profits without the note.

There is a strategy called a "wrap around mortgage" which has similar attributes to the sandwich lease and belongs in this discussion. With a wrap around, the investor buys the property using owner financing or a subject to arrangement and then re-sells the property using owner financing. It's basically the owner financing version of the sandwich lease. As you can probably guess though, in most cases, we strongly recommend avoiding this arrangement because if your new buyer stops paying, you'll have to foreclose.

Some investors have employed a solution whereby they put the deed in escrow and therefore if the homeowner stops paying even one payment on a wrap around mortgage, the deed in escrow can be recorded and the investor gets owner-ship of the property back. This is still not as wise of a move as simply offering a rent to own to the prospective buyer. When it comes to selling real estate, either get all (or as much as you can) at the closing or provide the new buyer with a rent to own arrangement so that you can maintain ownership and evict if the person stops paying you.

The "subject to", the lease purchase and owner financ-ing are three creative ways to buy real estate. Each state has different laws pertaining to these techniques so consult your real estate attorney before finalizing the paperwork on any of these types of deals.

Traditional Purchase

As always, you can buy real estate the old fashioned way by bringing your money or someone else's money to the closing and actually purchasing real estate the traditional way. For many people, this is the only way they know how to acquire property. For our students, it's just one strategy in a series of ways in which to invest in real estate. The biggest risk with purchasing real estate the traditional way is that it requires real money (either your own or someone else's). Anytime you are making the commitment to buy real estate with real money you are making a very big step and whether it is your money or not, it is a very big decision. In fact, the only thing worse than losing your own money, is losing someone else's money.

There are many places where purchasing real estate the traditional way can be applied very successfully because for some sellers, they just want to be fully cashed out and if you can provide that, you can sometimes be rewarded mightily for the service. Auctions are one of the primary places where purchasing property traditionally can be applied success-fully, including private auctions, REO/bank auctions and even foreclosure auctions. If the auction is "absolute" mean-ing they will take the highest bidder no matter what, so long as you aren't competing with several of other bidders, you may be able to pick up an incredible deal. Be cautious about getting emotional in these situations as that is how auction-eers make their living, preying on the emotions of bidders.

Another common use of this strategy is with free and clear property owners who are not interested in owner financing but want to turn their real estate into quick cash. This is prevalent with probate situations and property ac-quired through inheritance. Some owners have beneficiaries specified in a will which makes the transfer much simpler than when the real estate has not been estate planned and therefore must go through the probate system. Those people that acquire real estate through inheritance are sometimes very motivated to turn their new real estate holdings into cash and are willing to take far less than value to have the money quick.

Another solid deal finding technique that lends itself to the traditional purchase technique is sending out large numbers of automated offers to properties for sale. With this concept, the investor submits low ball offers to site unseen real estate in the hopes that a small percentage of owners may either agree or counteroffer. Usually, the offer amount is 50% or so of the list price. If just 0.1% responds positively, so long as you have a large number of properties to send offers to, this technique can be highly productive.

Since most beginning real estate investors do not have piles of money lying around the house, most who want to participate in purchasing real estate the traditional way must line up other people's money. The traditional way is to go to your local bank or mortgage broker and borrow the money from them. Qualifying for an investor, or "non-owner occu-pied" loan, from a mortgage company or bank can be very challenging, even for those with plenty of cash and good credit. Mortgage companies and banks may be a bit more lenient during boom cycles than downturns in the market, but almost always they will require sourced and seasoned down payment funds (you can prove where the down pay-ment came from and that you have had it for 90 days or more), a strong credit rating and plenty of income to offset the debt payment.

Even if your plan is to rent the property to a tenant, most mortgage companies and banks will not recognize the prospects of future income on that property in your income calculation. In other words, they will want you to qualify as if you were going to purchase the property and leave it sitting there vacant for 30 years. And after all of this trouble, the interest is usually much higher than if you were moving into the home to live in it. Plus, they rarely offer to roll property improvement expenses into the loan, so either you purchase real estate that requires no fix up work or you find some other source to fund the renovations. As you can see, there are numerous hurdles to obtaining a traditional mortgage for an investment property from a bank or mortgage company. Still, for some investors, they can walk through the hoops required for non-owner occupied conventional loans and this is one option for securing other people's money for a purchase outright deal.

Another other people's money source for you includes "hard money lenders" which are private lenders that lend money based on the value of the property as opposed to your financial position. Instead of proving income, your cash position and credit score, the deal finances itself. This also means that you must have a terrific deal on your hands. Typically hard money lenders loan up to 65% of the fair market value of the property. Further, their definition of fair market value is usually extremely conservative. A more realistic rule of thumb when searching for hard money is that they will lend 60% of fair market value. As you can see, you really need to secure an incredible deal to be able to utilize hard money.

Hard money also has one more major bonus besides not being borrower driven. You can borrow the money to renovate the property as well. They will usually distribute these funds in draws as work is completed. If the hard money lender is local, he or she may set up a schedule whereby they review the progress once per week and then cut a draw check based on the amount of work completed.

WISDOM KEY: Although hard money lenders will allow some of their funds to be used to improve the property, they usually do not allow you to borrow the money in which to cover the monthly payments. What some investors do to get around this rule is to obtain more from the weekly draw than is needed to cover the expenses and over the course of a month, build up enough in order to make each month's payment. This strategy may prove to be detrimental if the hard money lender finds out and their trust with you is immediately broken. Also, the draw checks usually do not continue to flow forever. Therefore, anytime you make the decision to use hard money, have some cash in reserves to cover monthly payments. Just because hard money will usually cover the upfront amount to buy the property as well as the renovation expenses, this doesn't necessarily mean it's a "no cash no credit" type deal.

As markets flow up and down, hard money lenders come and go as well. During boom times, some hard money lenders will extend across state lines and even provide funding nationwide. But during bust times, usually the nationwide hard money lenders disappear and the only ones left making these types of loans are local people who know their markets very well. The typical charge for their hard money can vary but most have both a fee component and an annual interest rate. Hard money lenders usually charge a 3% to 5% fee upfront and an interest rate of 15% per year. Develop relationships with local hard money lenders. Once you have developed strong relationships, then the lending guidelines may loosen up and you may be able to get more favorable terms. The key to harvesting hard money lenders is doing a few deals that work out real well for them. The more great deals you do, the better the relationship will be.

Other private money sources may include friends and family who have self-directed IRAs or other liquid assets who are interested in what they consider to be the safe and consistent returns real estate provide over the volatile stock market. There are numerous rules and regulations surrounding using other people's money that must be adhered to before you should embark on using your uncle's nest egg.

The benefits of using friends and family funds is the ease with which it can sometimes be obtained, the flexibility with which the money can be used and the terms that you can negotiate. The negative is that you must be conservative with their funds because money has a way of destroying lifelong relationships if not handled properly. And when life is all said and done, your relationships will be far more valuable to you than your bank account.

Additional private money sources include wealthy individuals looking to make high safe and secure returns on their capital. This can include professional athletes, attorneys, doctors and corporate executives. To obtain funds from these sources, not only do you have to be conservative, you must also be professional. Typically, those with more money in life are wise enough to hold onto it and they typically avoid turning over large sums of their capital to just anyone. This system will also provide you with resources on how to build credibility so that you can tap into this gigantic source of potential private funds.

It is best to have only one private funding source per deal. When you pool other people's money together into one deal, you cross a threshold that involves the Securities and Exchange Commission (SEC) as well as a host of other departments and organizations that you probably didn't realize even existed. For most individual, private investors such as yourself, you will probably only need one or two wealthy individuals that can fully fund each deal personally and therefore would never be pooling numerous other people's money into one investment.

Purchasing real estate the traditional way involves only two major components; the purchase price and the funding source. The first component is fairly simple to understand; the lower the price you can buy the property for, the better. Anything over 80% of fair market value is usually very risky from a short term investing standpoint. It is far better to be more selective in the beginning, opting to only buy properties that you can purchase for less than 70% of fair market value.

The second component can be far more complex since there is so many different ways in which to fund a purchase. Further, your funding options will greatly increase as the deal gets better. If you can buy a property for 40% of the fair market value, money sources will come out of the wood work. If you have a deal at 85% of value, your money sources may be non-existent. Therefore, it's usually not a lack of money sources that will be the issue for you, but the weakness of the deal.

Buying real estate the traditional way will always be an effective strategy but it requires using real money to purchase the property and a low purchase price. Rather than only being able to apply this technique, it is far more productive to have this as one arrow in your large and expanding quiver of investing strategies.

Notes

The only other major niche within the real estate investing world is the buying and selling of notes. A "note" in this context is better known as a "mortgage note". When someone borrows money, he/she typically signs a "note" which specifies the amount and terms of the loan. Just like real estate, these notes can be bought and sold. The types of notes that are ideal for private investors like you to trade are those that were originated through an owner financing deal.

If you sold one of your deals to a buyer and owner financed the purchase, although you may have been happy with the monthly income at first, overtime, you may become motivated to turn that note into one lump sum of cash. If your note is "performing", meaning the borrower is paying on time each month, that note can be sold to a note buyer. (For non-performing notes, those too can be sold, but usually at a drastic discount.) Note buyers determine the amount they will pay for a note based on the interest rate the note carries, the down payment amount the borrower put down and also how long the borrower has been paying on the note. The more "seasoned", or longer, the note has been paid on time, the more marketable the note is. Also, the interest rate plays a very important role in the marketability of a note as well. For most note buyers, a financial calculator is their best friend. They factor in all of the details of the note and then come up with a number of which they are willing to pay.

As an investor, you can either buy notes (if you are sitting on some liquid assets) or you can trade them. Much like real estate, the more motivated the note holder, the better the deal you can negotiate. As a note trader, or "wholesaler", the most valuable skill you must develop is to know how much a note buyer will pay for a note. Once you know exactly how to calculate that number, you can then negotiate with the note holder a number lower what your note buyer will pay and thereby create a spread for you to profit. Much like finding a traditional wholesale deal, the more note holders you contact, the more likely you are to run into a motivated note seller and the more likely you are to put together a great deal.

Part 5: Your Real Estate Future

"If one advances confidently in the direction of his dreams, and endeavors to live the life which he has imagined, he will meet with a success unexpected in common hours." — Henry David Thoreau

Are you experiencing information overload at this point? Be proud of yourself, you have covered a lot of ground. Take a deep breath. Take another one. Feel better, now? Great. It's time to turn your attention to your real estate future.

After reading about all those different techniques for succeeding in real estate, you may be asking yourself, "Where do I start?" That is a very good question. Unfortunately, most people decide on which investing strategy to get started with using the guess and test approach. These individuals would probably not refer to their plan as a "guess" because they usually spend considerable time evaluating what to do. The problem is that oftentimes they are asking the wrong questions and not incorporating the right factors into their decision.

What typically happens with the guess and test approach is that a new investor will start investing with a strategy that they have determined to be the right technique at the right time. Some guess correctly the first time and they live happily ever after. Most don't. For the majority of budding investors, after choosing the wrong strategy, they experience some failures and then proceed to give up.

Would you like a better way to approach real estate investing that can prevent this undesirable outcome? Would you like a way to develop a plan that will work every time?

You're in luck. You obtained this book and then went one step forward and have read to this point. That was a very smart move. You're about to discover a very unique and extremely powerful way to determine where to get started investing in real estate. You probably have never read something quite like this before. Are you ready?

The best way to approach real estate investing involves creating a plan based on who you are, where you want to go and what you want to do. Rather than choosing which real estate techniques to employ based simply on where you think the most money is being made right now, instead, you take a much deeper assessment and determine the very best strategies to employ based on several factors. In other words, as opposed to letting real estate dictate your approach, you dictate which style of investing fits you best. Since there are so many different ways to invest, you have the power to choose.

When you choose your approach wisely, you prepare yourself for long term success. Much like the children's fable of the tortoise and the hare, slow and steady wins the race. Another analogy that applies to this concept is when someone is trying to improve their physical health. Most people who go on a diet, or begin an exercise program, or attempt any new way of improving their physical health typically give up before they begin to experience lasting results. Lasting weight reduction, or muscle tone, or whatever the health goal is, usually doesn't materialize in the first 30 days. Instead, the best results begin to appear after several months.

Therefore, if someone is changing their eating habits or increasing their exercise activity in an attempt to lose weight or to improve their overall health, it is very important that whatever program or plan they attempt, they stick to it for an extended period of time. For someone looking to lose weight by changing their eating habits or more exercise, it is far better to choose foods and exercises that they enjoy doing rather than foods they can barely swallow and exercise that they dread. The same is true with real estate, choose your approach wisely to ensure lasting results.

Creating Your Plan

Most successful businesses had a plan before they began. On the other hand, those who fail to plan, plan to fail. In order for you to be successful, you need a plan. Crafting your real estate investing plan will require thought and reflection. This section will walk you through several key questions to help guide you through the process of putting together your plan.

Entrepreneurs are often encouraged to write out a detailed business plan when first starting a business. There is usually a standard format and it can be several pages in length. The challenge with using a standard business plan format is that it may create more confusion than clarity. You aren't writing this plan for a venture capitalist or banker. You are putting this plan together for yourself. You want simplicity so that you can remember your plan without having to read through several pages. You want to know your plan and the best way to have it engrained in your mind is to keep it simple.

The ultimate business plan is one that is so simple, it can be written out on a napkin. My plan was written on a Southwest Airlines napkin while I was on a flight and looking down at all the houses below from my window seat. That napkin still sits on my desk to this day (although it has had some close calls when the cleaning lady has mistaken it for trash!) Getting your plan to the point of such clarity and simplicity that you can write it out on a napkin may require some time and mental energy. However, it will be well worth the reflection and thought to get your plan so clear that you write it out with a few words, boxes and arrows.

Your real estate investing plan should be deeply personal to you. It is *your* plan and no one else's. Just like you are different from everyone else, your plan will be slightly different from anyone else's.

I heard an interesting story about a guy who was jogging on his normal route one Saturday morning when after turning onto a particular street, he saw people lining the sidewalks that were cheering for him. He turned around and saw runners coming up behind him from a distance. He figured out that he had jogged right into a real road race that was going on and the crowd thought he was leading the pack! In a few blocks, his route took him off the road race onto a quiet street that led back to his house. Although the crowd created a temptation for him to stay in the direction of the road race, he maintained his course. He didn't go in the direction other people wanted him to go. He stuck to his plan.

We all have different plans and at times, you may have other people in your life try to tell you what your plan needs to be. In the long run, you will be far happier and better off following your plan rather than following what other people want you to do with your life. Develop your own plan and then stick to that plan.

At core of becoming a real estate investor is in knowing what you want real estate to do for you and what life you want for yourself. The last thing you want to do is achieve a milestone that you never wanted to reach in the first place. Knowing what you want is the first step in achieving anything. Once you know your destination, then you can begin determining how to get there.

The most successful people envision what they want before they begin. Oftentimes the main reason why someone feels like they are not reaching their full potential in life has far less to do with effort and ambition and far more to do with not having thought about where they want to end up. Commit to spending the mental time and energy necessary to figure out where it is you want to go. It will be some of the best thinking you've ever done and it may be among the most productive time you have spent on creating a better life for yourself.

Goals

Goals are extremely powerful. Numerous studies have proven that when you set a goal you are actually crafting your future in advance. When you set goals correctly, you'll be amazed at just how incredibly powerful goals can be in your life.

In my own experiences, setting goals has created some extraordinary and surprisingly results. To illustrate, I remember being in my truck, homeless, and I wrote out some goals, including that I wanted to go surfing. I had no idea how I was going to go surfing since I was in Nashville, TN, hundreds of miles from the closest ocean. I had no real plan for how to do it. I had never been surfing before. I had no money and no good prospects for making any money at the time I wrote out the goal. All I had was a goal and a burning desire to achieve that goal. Exactly one year from the date I wrote down the goal of surfing, I was surfing in Pacifica, CA, just south of San Francisco. Although that is a small example, it shows that setting goals is how you can craft your future in advance.

Set some 1 year (immediate), 3 years (near future) and 10 years (long term) goals. They can be specific to real estate investing but also to your life in general. Take your time and allow yourself to dream. You may want to pick a quiet time when there are no other distractions. Make your goals as specific as possible and make sure there is a time frame for each one. Don't limit yourself to ideas that you know are very easy to attain. Think big. You can chose to remove the ones you don't really care that much about later. When you are setting goals, let your imagination run free.

Next, prioritize these goals based on which ones generate the most emotions inside of you. The way you ensure you achieve your goals is to anchor powerful emotions to them. You accomplish this by applying the principle of pain and pleasure. You want to associate positive, pleasurable emotions to achieving your goals and negative, painful emotions to not reaching them. Here's how you do this, step by step, for each goal.

First, picture all of the wonderful things that will happen once you have achieved the goal. Really think about it so that you can feel the pleasure. Smile while you are picturing this wonderful world with your goal achieved. This may take practice and you may have to do this several times to really start to attach, or associate positive emotions to reaching your goals.

Second, you need to associate pain to not achieving that goal. What would it feel like if you didn't reach this goal? Don't skip this step because this is actually more important than the pleasurable emotion step. People will do far more to avoid pain than to gain pleasure. Therefore, attaching negative emotions to not achieving your goals will motivate you more than pleasurable feelings.

Thinking negative is not always easy for people. We are often encouraged to think positive so thinking negative may take some getting used to. A productive way to create intense negative emotions about not reaching your goals involves picturing what your life would be like if you didn't achieve your plans. What if you life is the exact same as it is right now 1 year from now? What about 3 years from now? How about a full 10 years from now? What would it feel like to have the exact same situation in life a decade from now? It may not be fun to think negatively but this is how you program your mind for success. The more painful your picture is of not achieving your goals, the better.

A great example of this was expressed in the Charles Dickens' classic involving Ebenezer Scrooge. Scrooge was haunted by three ghosts; the ghost of Christmas past, present and future. Do you remember which ghost was the most influential in getting Scrooge to change? The ghost of Christmas future was. Why? It created the most pain for Scrooge. Seeing his future if he continued to live the same way he had been living was so frightening (painful), that he made permanent changes to his behavior.

Give yourself the gift of your own Scrooge experience. It may not be fun but you will be very thankful you took the time to draw out the pain because the pain is what is going to drive you. Your goals need to be emotionalized or they will not be effective and negative emotions associated with not reaching your goals will be the most powerful.

The goals that do not generate emotions are the ones you want to remove from your goals list. Prioritize your goals based on what is most important to you. When you complete this goal setting experience, you want your goals list to be a set of items that gets you highly emotional every time you think about them. The more emotion you attach to your goals, the more likely you will achieve them.

WISDOM KEY: Why does goal setting work? Studies have shown that the same areas of the brain are activated when you envision and when you actually experience that activity in the real world. That means, you can actually practice something without having to physically do it! For example, a study was done involving basketball players whereby one group was asked to picture shooting free throws successfully, another group was asked to actually shoot free throw shots and the third group was asked to do nothing. Then, the three groups were tested by shooting free throws. Guess who shot the best percentage? You're right, the ones that pictured themselves successfully shooting free throws. How? The same areas of the brain are activated whether the subjects were physically shooting the free throws or simply envisioning they were. The difference was that the ones who were envisioning the shots, were picturing the ball going in successfully. By the way, this free throw shot experiment involved experienced basketball players. Don't expect to be able to master a skill that involves muscle memory such as shooting a basketball from the free throw line by simply envisioning it. You do have to actually do it as well to teach your muscles how to do it. When it comes to setting your goals, envision what you want. If you do it long enough, with enough emotion, your brain will begin to think that it is achieving the goal you have set and you'll be amazed at the results.

What's Your Perfect Day of Play?

If you could have a day to do whatever you wanted (non-work related), what would be your perfect day of play? Where would you be, who would you be with and what would you be doing? Get a very clear mental picture of this day. Some have used cut-out pictures from magazines or copied images online to put together a collage, or vision board, to help them see their perfect day of play.

You want to experience as many senses in envisioning your perfect day of play as possible. For example, my perfect day of play is on the beach. When I would envision this place, not only would I look at beach pictures, I also would have a breaking waves audio playing, some beach sand in my hand and I would even open up a bottle of sunscreen. By doing this, my experience would include several senses beyond just sight, including sound, touch and smell.

Then, as you have already learned, you must associate emotions to your perfect day of play. Emotion creates motion.

What's Your Perfect Day of Work?

What does your perfect day of work look like? Have you ever even thought about that before? Most people who dream about a better life typically only focus on things they would do if they didn't have to work; vacations, travel, debt-free, time with loved ones, etc. You also need a clear mental picture of what your ideal day of work would be like.

Believe it or not, when you are financially able to do nothing, you won't be doing nothing. How do I know this? Humans are programmed to be happier and more fulfilled when they have something to do. Sure, you might work less, but when you reach your financial goals, you will probably still be working on some project, idea, cause or business. Perhaps you will be fighting some injustice in the world, or growing a massive financial empire to pass down to your children or maybe just helping people, one deal at a time. Be prepared for the day when you are financially free by also envisioning your perfect day of work.

Did your perfect day of work vision include real estate? Is real estate a means to an end or is it part of your end? It's OK either way; you can't have a wrong answer here because this is all about you. Maybe your plan is to make a whole bunch of money in real estate now so that you can finance a lifetime pursuing your true passion. Or possibly, you want to be a real estate tycoon in your perfect day of work? Which brings us to this important question...

Full Time or Part Time?

Do you want real estate to eventually be a full time business for you or do you envision real estate as being a part time endeavor while you focus the bulk of your working life on another career? Some people love what they do for a living and real estate is just an on-the-side activity; a way to build long term financial security. For others, quitting their job is on the forefront of their mind. Real estate can be a wonderful career as well as a great side business. Do you want real estate to eventually be full time or part time?

Small Fast Cash, Big Slow Money or Long Term Wealth?

What do you need real estate to do for you right now? Do you need some quick extra money in your bank account immediately? Do you have plenty of money and simply want to get a better return on your investing dollar? Are you doing just fine financially and have the ability to patiently await large profit checks in the next 6 months or so? You may be tempted to want to pursue all three at the same time; fast cash, slow big money and long term wealth. Although you can, in the beginning, it is better to choose one. Do you need money right now, can you wait it out to get even bigger money several months down the road or are you looking to build long term wealth?

Where?

Where do you want to invest? In your own backyard, halfway across the globe, everywhere? Thinking big is a great attribute. Thinking to broad when it comes to choosing where you want to invest rarely produces good results. Therefore, have big dreams, but also have clearly defined plans. This is very applicable to investors determining where they want to invest. For most investors, starting in their own area is ideal. However, in some cases, they may want to invest in another geographic location because they may have family there, or they heard the market is good there or maybe they will be moving there. You have to start some- where. The best place is usually in your own backyard. You can absolutely invest long distance as well. Where are you going to invest?

What Are Your Assets?

There are several types of assets that can be of great value to a real estate investor. The first, and most obvious, is your own personal financial situation. Are you in a similar spot that I was in when I first got started? No job, no cash, no credit, no retirement account, no house and only a car that had no equity in it? That's a tough place to begin. It drastically limits your options on what deals you can invest in.

Even if you aren't flush with cash in a bank account right now, do you have decent credit? Do you have a job that brings in steady W2 income? Do you have a retirement account? Do you have a home that may have some equity in it or other assets that may have some value? Get a complete assessment of your financial picture. You may be better off than you think. Every little bit helps increase the number of options you have available to you.

A less obvious, but extremely important asset you have is your network. Who do you know that may have a strong financial situation? People you know may have inherited money, accumulated a large retirement account or simply have cash, may be looking to get better returns on their money and your real estate deals can be a perfect opportunity to help them improve how hard their money is working for them (and help you do more deals). When you think about it, you may be surprised at the resources available to you. Who do you know?

What if you don't know anyone? That's OK too. The important thing is that you thought about it. And although no one may be coming to mind right now, overtime, a few people may pop into your head.

Another asset is your previous experience in real estate. What other deals have you done in the past? Are you in the real estate business already? Real estate agents and appraisers who want to become investors have a tremendous advantage and their current vocation is a great asset. Even if you haven't done your first deal yet or are not in the real estate business, have you read other books, gone to seminars or purchased courses? Your previous real estate education can be an asset as well.

If you have tried to invest in the past and failed, that's an asset too! Discovering what didn't work can be of great value. What real estate investing experiences (even if they are painful to reflect upon) have you had?

Take inventory on your assets. Knowing where you are starting form is extremely helpful in developing your plan. And if the mere thought of assessing your assets gets you upset over what you feel is a lack of assets, get excited because that is the kind of negative emotions that you can use to drive you to succeed. After reading this book, you'll never look at negative emotions quite the same way again!

Personality Type

Have you ever taken a personality test before? Do you know what personality type (or types) you are? The very best personality test results come from several people you know completing it for you. Discover more about yourself than you ever knew, have 3 people that know you very well complete a personality test for you.

Choosing Your Niche

What are the best strategies for you to pursue in real estate? Now that you have completed the previous self reflection questions, you can incorporate what you have determined about yourself into the real estate strategies you pursue. The following are some general guidelines to help you fit real estate into your plans. There are certainly going to be exceptions to the below guidelines but this is a great start for you:

Wholesales

- Makes fast cash but usually the profits are small compared to other techniques.
- Requires time and a commitment to finding motivated sellers and buyers. Very hands on. Those who want someone else to do all the work for them would not do well here.
- Works better in lower price point areas of town or in areas that do not have extremely high sales prices on starter homes. It can be very difficult to find wholesale opportunities with luxury or high end properties.
- Can be a people business because in order to put together a wholesale, you need to negotiate deals with buyers and sellers.
- Virtually risk free. You're biggest exposure would be your time.
- Opportunities come and go quickly with wholesales so you must be available to move when opportunity strikes.

Commissions / Fees

- Can produce fast and steady cash.
- Being a real estate agent or mortgage person is very much a people business whereas being an appraiser or inspector is not.
- Requires getting a license in most cases which can be time consuming and costly to acquire.
- Can become a career and a full time business for you.
- Can be done with little or no money (after you have paid to be licensed) and no credit.

Pre Foreclosures

- You can make fast cash, slow big money or long term wealth with Pre Foreclosures.
- You should have a heart for helping people to invest in pre foreclosures because you are dealing with people in distress.
- Each state has different laws surrounding how you handle sellers in pre foreclosure and states vary on foreclosure laws. Some states are far better for this technique than others.
- It really helps if you have access to some money because oftentimes the best deals involve a seller wanting a few thousand dollars to walk away. If you can write a check on the spot, you can sometimes get the deal of a lifetime.
- Like wholesales, Pre Foreclosures come and go quickly so you must be available to move when opportunity strikes.
- Can be done with little or no money and no credit.

Short Sales

- Takes significant time to get paid but sometimes the payoffs can be substantially larger.
- Good for an analytical mind because it involves a lot of numbers and calculating and a lot less dealing with people.
- You can make slow big profits or build long term wealth with this technique.
- Works best with higher priced properties (opposite of wholesales). The more expensive and luxurious the property, the more money you can make. The amount of time, energy and work required to do a luxury short

sale is the exact same as a short sale on a tiny starter home.

- Great for people with very little free time that have hectic schedules that change often. Short sales move slow and you can work them at your own pace.
- Can be done with little or no money and no credit.

Foreclosures

- Typically a slow big profit technique, although you can also build long term wealth with it.
- Requires money, especially for an earnest deposit and maybe even for a down payment.
- May require the ability to obtain a standard bank loan. Foreclosure listings often require the buyer pre-qualify for a loan before submitting an offer.
- You may be able to obtain a Hard Money loan to purchase a foreclosure but you would have to find either a non-listed deal or get very lucky and find a steal on a listed foreclosure since Hard Money loans rarely lend above 65%.
- For those who know people who have money they want to invest, foreclosures can be accessible for them as well.
- Significant risk is involved since you are buying the property with real money. You must know exactly what you are getting yourself into or you can lose money.
- Excellent for those who want to hire other people to do all the work for them; from finding the deal (a real estate agent), to assessing the value (an appraiser), to understanding the condition of the property (an inspector), to buying the property (mortgage person and closing company), to fixing it up (contractor), to sell-

ing it (listing agent.) Oftentimes, a multitude of people earn a living when an investor buys a foreclosure.

- Although foreclosures exist almost everywhere, some areas have more than others. The larger the supply of foreclosures, the more likely you can find a good deal.
- Good for a non-people person or an analytical person. The seller is a bank and there is very little emotion involved in the negotiation. It's strictly numbers.

Tax Deeds

- Typically a slow big profit technique, although you can also build long term wealth with it.
- Very similar characteristics to foreclosures because a tax deed sale is a form of a foreclosure sale.
- Requires money or access to money. Won't be able to use a loan in most cases because it is an auction.
- You must know the property and the area where the property is located very well.
- Buying real estate at auction is best for experts who have been in the business a long time.
- Not a people business at all. Strictly numbers.

Rehabs

- Great for people who like to fix, build or design. Some people gain tremendous satisfaction from transforming an ugly property into a beautiful one.
- Excellent for people who already have a background in construction or general contracting.
- Requires using real money to not only purchase, but also pay for the costs to renovate the property. You can use Hard Money loans, money from private sources, your own capital or even certain bank loans.

- In order to do one of these deals without your own cash or credit, you would need to get a Hard Money loan or use a private funding source.
- Considerable risk can be involved with these deals because not only is it possible to pay too much for the property, it is also possible that you could spend too much in renovation or during your repair work you could uncover unplanned problems that put you over budget.
- If you aren't going to do the work yourself, you need to hire and manage contractors, which is a skill all to itself. Strong people management skills may be necessary if you hire other to do the fix up work.
- Some investors rehab and resell while others choose to renovate just enough to make it rentable and then turn the property into a long term buy and hold rental.
- Oftentimes beginners start with a rehab project and it usually takes twice as long as they expected and they make half as much as they predicted. This strategy is better suited for intermediate to expert level investors due to all the pitfalls that you could run into.

Traditional Purchase

- Several strategies involve the use of a traditional purchase, include foreclosures, rehabs, and even sometimes short sales. Typically, a traditional purchase is a slow big profit technique, although you can also build long term wealth with it too.
- Great for people who do not have the time or the patience to educate themselves on real estate. They can simply hire a real estate agent to find them property

to buy. It is more hands off but you typically don't get as good of a deal.

- Requires cash, credit or both.
- This is how most people invest in real estate. It works, but it can be risky as well since you are buying property with real money, or using your credit.
- In certain situations, the only way to acquire the property is through a traditional purchase. If the deal is good enough, it may be worth it to go the traditional route.

Buy and Hold

- Not a fast cash producing experience. In fact, oftentimes it is extremely delayed gratification. Sometimes it can take several years to achieve any financial rewards.
- Great for building long term financial security and generating highly tax advantaged income.
- Not ideal for the personality that likes to do something for a short time and then move on to another project. Owning real estate long term is a long term commitment. It may require small bits of your time consistently for years.
- Significant level of risk since a property could go down in value or a tenant could inflict substantial damage as well as legal hassles.

Creative Finance - Lease Purchase, Subject To & Owner Financing

- Very much a people business.
- You need to be able to take rejection well since this requires a bit of sales skills to negotiate these deals.

- Great for those who want to build long term wealth but have no cash or credit.
- Like wholesales and Pre Foreclosures, these deals come and go quickly so you must be available to move when opportunity strikes.
- Typically works better in starter home areas and places that do not have high real estate prices

Tax Lien Certificates

- Once purchased, the investment is hands off and passive.
- Requires real money; either your own or a money resource. Mortgages are not originated on tax lien certificates so credit is not necessary; but cash is.
- A very analytical technique; an individual with strong interpersonal skills would not be able to put their strengths to any use here.
- Very much delayed gratification. It can take several years for a tax lien certificate investment to mature.
- For those with tons of money but no time, this can be a great way to invest in real estate. Oftentimes people move some of their retirement funds to a self directed IRA and buy tax lien certificates with their retirement money.

Notes

- Note buying requires money, either you own or someone else's. Some investors wholesale notes, which is a form of wholesaling described earlier.
- Since you are buying a mortgage when you buy a note, you don't need credit since you aren't getting a mortgage to buy a mortgage.

- Not a people business. Very analytical. A financial calculator is your Notes advisor.
- In fact, it can be very non-people oriented. One of the main activities of a Note buyer is collections. Although you can hire another company to be the primary collections contact to the borrower, you still have to manage that collections company.
- Investing in Notes involves significant collections activities. If you are a soft person when it comes to tough business decisions, this may not be the avenue for you.
- Can create excellent long term revenue.

This brief overview of the differences between each of the main ways to invest in real estate will hopefully provide you with ideas on how to begin to create your investing plan. One of the most important tasks our team is faced with when we add a new apprentice is determining the best plan for that person. Since real estate changes so much, and each person is so different, it usually takes considerable thought to put together a truly effective plan. Therefore, if it takes us, the experts on the subject, substantial time to get it right, don't assume you're plan is going to be completed in short order.

Take your time with this process. Allow yourself to reflect and ponder. Abraham Lincoln is quoted as having said, "If I was given 8 hours to chop down a tree, I would spend the first 7 sharpening the blade." Ultimately, you want all that thought to culminate into a plan that has been so thoroughly thought through that you can write on a napkin.

Now What?

Congratulations, you made it to the end of the book! That is a significant milestone. You are a finisher in a world of starters.

Becoming a real estate investor is not a destination. It's a journey. On this journey, you'll learn about real estate, how to make money and also about yourself. Be your own biggest encourager. Don't beat yourself up when things don't work out as you planned. Instead, recognize that any challenges that you encounter is all part of the journey. So enjoy the journey!

Have fun with figuring out how to be a real estate investor. Life's too short to be too serious. Have a sense of humor and laugh along the journey. When things are incredibly good, remember that the highs are part of the ride. When things are not-so-good, keep in mind that the lows are a part of the journey as well.

Continually educate yourself while you are taking action. Don't use education as a reason to not get started. Instead, use education to enhance your progress. Read books (I have added some recommendations in Appendix B), invest in courses, take classes and most importantly, get a mentor. If you never stop learning more about real estate investing, you'll never stagnate and you'll continue to grow personally and financially.

Believe you can succeed. As Henry Ford said, "Whether you think you can or you think you can't, you're right." Your actions will always follow your beliefs. Believe you can be a real estate investor.

Here's your next step...go take action! Don't be like the majority of people in this world that allow fear to stop them from pursuing their dreams. Have the courage to step out of your comfort zone and go after the life which you have imagined. This is the first day of the rest of your life. You only live once. Make the most of it.

> As you can probably tell, I put a tremendous amount of time, effort and passion into writing this book. Although I am a bit biased, I sincerely believe that anyone looking to be a real estate investor should read this book. If you think this book would be of value to other people who are interested in becoming real estate investors, can you recommend this book to them? Let your social media outlets know about it. Tell whomever you think would enjoy reading it. There is no monetary or other financial gain for doing so. You would be doing this out of the goodness of your heart and as a favor to me. I want to thank you in advance for letting others know about this book.

I want to personally thank you for taking the time to read this book. I pray that you will take the knowledge you have gained and apply it as soon as possible. Remember, action over analysis. There is no time like the present to take action. Thank you for reading and God bless.

How to be a Real Estate Investor

Appendix A - Building Your Team

Real estate is a team sport and to achieve long term success in real estate, you must have a great team. The secret to building a great team is to only work with the right people. There is a HUGE difference between the right people and the wrong people. Most people can find problems and point them out to you. The right team player for you may point out problems, but they will also point out ways to solve them. Instead of saying, "you can't do that," the right real estate team member would say, "you can't do it that way, but you can do it this way." Telling someone what can't be done requires far less effort, intelligence and creativity than telling him/her how it can be done. The right people are possibility thinkers that come up with solutions, not just problems.

Bad advice from the wrong team members has been detrimental to scores of budding real estate entrepreneurs. All it takes is just one bad apple, one piece of bad advice, one comment from the wrong person and some beginners may never become real estate investors. Usually, the bad advice or the potentially destructive comments sounds something like, "you can't do that," or even worse, "what you are trying to do is illegal."

It is heartbreaking to see prospective investors get discouraged, or even quit, as a result of a single comment from the wrong team member. Be very aware that bad advice from the wrong people is a very serious threat to your success. It has been one of the biggest ambition destroyers we have come across. And all it takes is one comment, one sentence, one suggestion; and you can be derailed from your mission.

How do you prevent this calamity from occurring? How do you avoid bad advice from the wrong people destroying your enthusiasm and ambition for becoming a real estate investor? In the beginning, before you really have a deep understanding of how real estate really works, only work with team members that are possibility thinkers. If they only point out problem but do not provide solutions as well, they are the wrong team members for you. Further, it would be far better to find people who are investor friendly and understand the entire world of creative real estate investing. And for goodness sake, if someone tells you what can't be done but can't offer up any ways it can be done; please, please, please have the courage to continue to seek a solution.

> **WISDOM KEY:** If you feel yourself trying to train a team member on what to do, you probably have the wrong team member on your hands. Sure, you may have to explain to the person what it is you are trying to accomplish, but you shouldn't have to teach them as well. In fact, the purpose of the team member is to teach you! You are looking for people that know infinitely more about there particular role than you do. When investors try to train narrow-minded, traditional real estate professionals on creative, out-of-the-box concepts, it usually ends poorly. People that are not possibility thinkers can get down right upset when you begin to try to reason with them on the merits of a creative idea. Let the non-possibility thinkers wallow in their narrow-mindedness. Focus on connecting with and learning from the right people, the possibility thinkers, the team players that come up with creative solutions.

Surround yourself with positive, encouraging and uplifting people. We live in a very negative world and when you are surrounded by negative people and influences, it can really wear on you. Plus, when you are embarking on a new journey, you are more vulnerable to negative influences than at any other time. It is when you are most unsure of yourself that negative comments can really take a foothold in your mind.

In this section, you're going to discover who the most important team members are going to be for your real estate investing business. In the beginning, you may only require one person for each but overtime, you should continually seek out and find more and more team members. After all, if one of your main team players is unavailable, you may need to bring in a substitute to finish the game.

Going out into the real world of real estate to meet with industry professionals like attorneys, agents, closing representatives and mortgage lenders; requires the proper mindset. There are many different people out there and the advice of the first person you meet with should not be held as absolute truth. In fact, you will find that if you ask 3 people the same question, you will get three different answers. Have the mindset that you will obtain different opinions from different people and avoid making big, real estate investing career altering decisions, based on one person's comments.

Closing Companies

Begin with the end in mind by making your first team member the company that is responsible for handling the closing of real estate transactions, closing companies. In some states, real estate transactions are closed by title companies while in others, attorneys handle the closings and still others use escrow companies, attorneys and title companies to close a transaction. To make it simple, we are going to refer to them as simply "closing companies".

The right closing company is the most important player on your team. If you have a lousy closing company, creative real estate investing can be a nightmare. But if you have the right one, creative real estate investing becomes possible and profitable.

You need a very investor friendly closing company; a group of people that handle creative investing closings every month. The vast majority of closing companies in your area are not investor friendly and do not handle creative closings. 90% of the closing companies you will come in contact with if you simply started dialing random companies out of a directory would not be a good fit for you. You are looking for the rare few, the minority of closing companies that have carved out a niche catering to real estate investors.

How do you find an investor friendly, creative investing competent closing company? Ask other successful investors in your area who they use to close their transactions. In every area, there is usually at least one closing company that almost every other investor uses to close their deals. You want to use the same company the other smart, successful and rich investors in your area are using.

The right closing company is the foundation of building a team. Once you have the right closing company, the rest of the team members will be much easier to locate.

Attorneys

You need a good real estate attorney. Real estate is full of rules, regulations and laws. Most professionals that serve the real estate industry know very little about how the actual rules, regulations and laws are written but most will act like they do. A smart real estate attorney will be able to separate fact from fiction for you. They will be able to make sure that you don't get yourself into any hot water while still transacting creative deals and making money. The right attorney will be a deal maker for you, not a deal breaker.

Your closing company is the first place to start in finding the right real estate attorney. In fact, many closing companies either are owned by attorneys or have attorneys working in their office. These attorneys know your local real estate world better than anyone else because they see closings every business day, day in and day out. They are in the trenches of the business more than any other attorneys. This is the best place to start your search.

The only challenge you may run into with attorneys that own or work for closing companies is that they may claim that they only handle real estate closings. In which case, you can ask for the name of the attorney they would recommend you use. By starting with the most investor friendly closing companies, even if the attorneys on staff cannot help you, they can direct you to an attorney who can.

Go local. National real estate attorneys may be helpful for broad or general topics, but what you need is someone local who knows all of the tiny nuisances for your specific area. The differences can be quite dramatic from one state to another. Stick with a local attorney. And go with a possibility thinking attorney; someone who comes up with ideas and ways for you to do something. Don't settle for advice such as, "it can't be done." You need attorney who can show you how it can be done.

If you have any intention of owning real estate and leasing it to tenants, you should have an eviction attorney on your team before you ever lease your first property. Landlord and tenant laws are county specific and the process by which a tenant is evicted can be markedly different from county to county. Therefore, you will need a separate eviction attorney for every county that you own real estate.

Thankfully, there is a gigantic short cut to locating a dynamite eviction attorney for each county and here it is. Call (or go in person to) the court clerk's office that processes all of the eviction filings for that county. Ask a very simple question. "Which eviction attorney names do you see most often on the docket?"

We have discovered that 10% of the eviction attorneys are handling 90% of the eviction cases in any given area. You want the names of top two or three attorneys. These are the attorneys that have offices situated next to the courthouse and literally everyday eviction court is in session, these attorneys are in attendance. They may process 10, 20 or even 30 or more evictions per court session. These are the same people that go hunting, or fishing or play golf with the eviction judge. In short, these eviction attorneys get evictions done faster and better than everyone else by a very large margin. They have the location, expertise, systems and judge relationships to get tenants out of properties as fast as the law will allow.

Once you have the names of the top two or three, call each office and find out if they will take single property eviction filings. The problem with some of these superstar eviction attorneys is that they only work with big clients such as large apartment complexes that have several eviction filings at a time. You need an attorney who has the capability to work with the singles as well. Be persistent. Usually at least one of the top eviction attorneys in a given area will take individual eviction filings.

If you have your closing attorney, local real estate attorney and superstar eviction attorney in place, you have your legal department complete. Putting this part of the team together is your first order of business when building your team.

Real Estate Agents

It may be extremely important that you build a relationship with at least one key real estate agent. But it may not. Because what you really need is not an agent at all, but actually, the capabilities a real estate agent possesses, including; access to MLS comps and the ability to list properties for sale on the MLS.

If you are already licensed (or you have a spouse with a license or you have a license in retirement), you have what you need already and you don't need to add a real estate agent to your team. You're done and can mark this off your team building checklist!

> **WISDOM KEY:** If, by chance, you are thinking of getting licensed, I'll save you some money and headaches by informing you that it is usually not a good use of your time and money to go and get your license until you have at least closed a few deals. Obtaining your license is expensive, extremely time consuming and will take away from your immediate goal of closing deals. Once you have made some good money, then you can go back and get your license if you so choose.

If you are not licensed and do not have a close family member or spouse who is licensed, you'll need to develop a key relationship with an agent who has access to the MLS. The residential real estate business revolves around this system called the MLS, or the Multiple Listing Service. It is a database of all of the properties for sale, as well those that have been sold. Appraisals are created from comparable sales found on the MLS so most valuations of real estate are based on the information gathered from the MLS. More than 90% of residential real estate is sold through the MLS. The MLS is so important for anyone dealing with residential real estate and a real estate agent is your key to the MLS.

The MLS is controlled by the National Association of Realtors® (NAR). In order for someone to get access to the MLS, in most cases, the NAR requires the person be a licensed real estate agent who pays the yearly and monthly fees to be a member of the National and Local Association of Realtors® and then a benefit of being a member includes MLS access.

Our lives as investors would be so much easier if we could simply pay a company a monthly fee to have access to the MLS. But the NAR thus far has not allowed that to happen. They guard the MLS mightily because it is their monopoly, their golden goose. If the NAR didn't own the MLS, real estate agents would be far less likely to pay their dues to remain members.

As an investor, you have two options for gaining MLS access. First, you could become an agent yourself, which is rarely a good option in the beginning but can be a great idea down the road. Second, you could get access through another real estate agent. They may not let you access it by yourself, but you can ask that agents to produce reports and search the system for you. This is what most investors do. They have a real estate agent on their team who helps them access MLS information and in exchange, the agent may get a commission on some the investor's transactions.

Here are some tips for locating your key agent relationship. First, you may want to stay away from extremely successful, top producing agents. They may not have the time or the patience to consistently provide you with what you need when you need it. You want to connect with an agent who is either part time, or struggling, or at the very least, not on a billboard or bus bench. Remember, for your key relationship, you don't necessarily need the assistance of a successful agent; you just need what only the MLS can provide. And almost every agent has MLS capabilities. Try asking around your church, or fitness center, or other civic club. Look for cards tacked to grocery bulletins or other community boards. Better yet, ask your circle of influence if anyone they know has their real estate license. You will be surprised who turns up with a license. One of our students found out that the person in the cubicle next to him had an active license but never used it. You never know.

DISCLAIMER: If you are a licensed real estate agent, please don't take offense to what you are about to read. The following is what we have experienced over a very long period of time of working and interacting with real estate agents.

Be very discerning of the advice you will get from real estate agents. The reason is because many are not qualified to provide you with accurate investing advice. Most agents are not real estate investors. The average agent earns at the bottom of the income scale and rents their home. In other words, many are broke and some have not even bought or sold a home themselves. Therefore, be very leery of taking advice on real estate investing from a broke person, even if they are a real estate agent.

Be aware that agents can be the #1 discourager of aspiring investors. Even with the best of intentions, they have been known to muffle an investor's ambition and completely eliminate his/her enthusiasm. It has been very disappointing and frustrating to watch over the years as well intentioned real estate agents that didn't truly know what they were talking about, discourage people from pursuing their dream of investing in real estate.

Sadly, you have probably learned more about making money with real estate by reading this book than most agents know. How is that possible? Most agents are not taught how to make money in real estate. The classes and the tests a real estate agent must complete to be licensed rarely mention how to make money; they focus on laws, rules, regulations and everything that an agent is NOT supposed to do. There is a very big difference between knowing what not to do and knowing how to make money. Therefore, most real estate agents are not given any education on how to really make it in real estate. They are given advice on how to be a licensed real estate agent.

Many real estate investors become frustrated with the agents they meet. Some have labeled agents as, "the most broke know-it-alls they have ever met." This sentiment comes from having done transactions with those agents that act like they know everything about the real estate business but yet are making barely above the poverty level in income. The question you want to ask any know-it-all is, "if you are so smart, how come you're not rich?"

There is no need to get upset and bothered by agents that clash with an investor's creative approach to real estate. It's not that agents are bad people; they are wonderful people. The problem is that many have not received the right education and they haven't been exposed to the right mentors. That's one of the reasons why the broke ones are so broke.

Agents are a very large part of the residential real estate world and you will be contact with them on almost every transaction you do. They handle the bulk of the real estate needs of buyers and sellers. As an investor, you are the outsider, you are the minority. Therefore, you need to appreciate and respect real estate agents. But you don't have to heed their advice on how to get rich with real estate if they are broke. You don't have to take legal advice from them either; that's what your attorney provides for you.

> **WISDOM KEY:** A very tiny percentage of agents are actually nothing like the majority. They are extremely successful. There are agents out there that make over $1,000,000 per year. These people have been given the right education and have had the right mentors. If you are fortunate enough to network and build relationships with these people, then you would be very wise to take advice from them. Top producing real estate agents are a wealth of knowledge. Since they are making a ton of money, they have the authority to provide you with advice on how to make money in real estate.

You need access to the MLS and the ability list a property for sale on the MLS. Agents are the gatekeepers to these items. If you are not already licensed, you will need the assistance of a helpful agent. Interacting with agents can be like walking through a minefield; you may have smooth sailing if you're lucky, but in most cases, you'll run into some not-so-fun conversations. The key is to remember that only rich and successful real estate professionals are qualified to provide useful advice on making money in real estate.

Mortgage People

You made it past the real estate agent section, excellent! Now we can move onto a more positive team player, mortgage people. Most real estate transactions involve a mortgage. Getting a buyer a mortgage is critically important because the mortgage feeds everyone else in the transaction. When a mortgage funds at a closing, it oftentimes pays for most, if not all, of the purchase, including the agent commissions, the attorney fees, the appraisal and of course, the seller. If the mortgage does not go through, no one gets paid. Therefore, the mortgage is a crucial part of almost every real estate transaction and those who originate mortgages should be very important members of your team.

There are three types of mortgage people you will need for your team. Although it is humanly possible that one mortgage person could fulfill all three types; usually you will need more than one. The first, and most important, is a no-title-seasoning mortgage person who knows how to get loans closed whereby the lender does not require title seasoning.

Title seasoning refers to the length of time the seller has been the owner of the property. In some deals, you may only be the owner, or "on title", for 30 days or less when you sell the property to the new buyer. Some mortgage companies have rules stating that the seller to the property must be the owner for more than 60, 90 even 180 days before they will lend money; also known as title seasoning restrictions.

You need access to mortgage options for new buyers that do not have title seasoning restrictions. Typically, portfolio lenders, or those lenders that originate and service their own loans, tend to have little to no issues with title seasoning. Local, regional and national banks are likely to be portfolio lenders and therefore should have mortgage divisions that service many of the loans they originate. Many of these lenders can originate loans that do not require title seasoning.

> **WISDOM KEY:** Most portfolio lenders charge very few fees and offer extremely low interest rates. This comes in handy when the buyer's original mortgage person can't get a no-title seasoning loan done and therefore the only way to keep the deal alive may be to move the buyer to your mortgage person. When your mortgage person is not only able to get the loan completed but is also very competitive in terms of fees and interest rate, you look like the hero in the deal because everyone gets paid when the loan is successfully funded by the mortgage company.

The second type of mortgage person you need on your team is someone who can get loans for first time homebuyers, those with less-than-perfect credit and those borrowers that don't fit into the standard loan program. These mortgage professionals should be well versed in closing government loans such as FHA, VA, local down payment assistance programs, local down payment grants and other local and federal government loan programs.

The first place to look to find these types of mortgage people is to seek out first time homebuyer home builders in your area. Most home builders are excellent at getting prospective buyers loans to purchase their properties. They have done the hard work of finding the right mortgage companies to help first time homebuyers become home owners. Look for the lowest priced new homes you can and call on those builders. Ask who they recommend for mortgages. Some may even have their in house mortgage team. As a general rule, the mortgage companies that service successful local builders of first time homebuyer homes are usually excellent for your team.

Hard Money Lenders

Some of the deals that you will come across may require the use of money in order for you to profit. You may not need to use your own money, but instead, you may be able to use other people's money. Most successful real estate investors have used other people's money to build their empire.

You want as many money sources as you can assemble. Get started by seeking out hard money lenders. A hard money lender lends money based on the merits of the deal and not on the merits of borrower. They cater to and lend money to investors.

The ideal terms of a hard money loan include financing the entire purchase including the closing costs, providing you a few thousand dollars at the closing to initiate any renovation work that may be needed and will periodically administer draws to you as work is completed. Hard money lenders that offer such terms do exist. They will usually lend no more than about 65% of fair market value so you must find great deals in order to work with them. Hard money lenders tend to be single person operations so developing a relationship with them will be critical. In some cases, you may be required to complete a few deals with a hard money lender to develop the working business relationship to a point where they feel comfortable enough to provide you with favorable terms.

With hard money loans, the interest rate is very high, ranging from 10% to as much as 20% in some cases. You do not need to be as concerned about the cost of borrowing the money if you have a great deal on your hands. Having the ability to buy a property without qualifying for a conventional loan may be far more valuable than the difference between paying 5% versus 15%. If you were able to purchase a property for $100,000 that could be resold for $150,000 after some repairs, would 15% interest on a $100,000 loan for a few months be all that bad? Would it be worse than not being able to do the deal at all?

Hard money lenders can be found by networking with other investors in your area. When communicating with them, ask good questions such as what they define as a perfect deal. Learn about their process and what they are looking for in a deal. Most importantly, do not come across as if you are begging for money. Instead, present yourself as an investor who works on great deals and that you may have a few excellent hard money opportunities in the near future. Many investors mistakenly assume they need to beg for deal money. Conversely, successful investors look at presenting a deal to a hard money lender as an opportunity. Be an opportunity presenter, not a money begger.

> **WISDOM KEY:** Hard money lenders with a long track record of lending money to investors in your area are extremely knowledgeable. You may find your hard money person to be one of your best consultants when contemplating whether to renovate and re-sell a deal or to simply traditional wholesale it to another investor. Plus, the more you communicate and seek advice from your hard money person, the more likely they will reach out to you for advice as well. This relationship can save you time and money by learning from the experiences of other local investors who wouldn't normally share their best lessons with you. Whereas other investors may perceive you as competition and therefore may resist sharing detailed local knowledge, hard money lenders usually don't have anything to lose by sharing what they have learned

because the smarter and more informed you are, the more likely they will make money from you.

General Contractors

Although you may not have any interest in renovating properties, you may need the assistance of a general contractor to help assess the costs to fix up properties as well as to be available to help you with odds and ends that may be required when you are buying and selling real estate. And if you want to buy dilapidated properties to fix up, a general contractor may be of tremendous help. These individuals should be licensed, insured and bonded professionals that also have worked with other real estate investors in the past.

GCs, as they are called, vary tremendously based on what jobs they typically work. Some focus on luxury home renovations with virtually unlimited budgets. These types of GCs usually do not fit well with real estate investors because the goal of most investors is to renovate the property to the level and standard of the other homes in the neighborhood. You wouldn't want Taj Majal level work in a starter level home. You are looking for a general contractor that can be very efficient and can stay at or below budget. The best way to determine this is to look at the last 3 jobs they did. The proof will be in the pudding.

General contractors also know other sub contractors and therefore, if you have a specific need that the GC isn't suited for, he/she will probably know someone who can help.

Tax Advisors

By now, if you have the right closing company, real estate attorney, real estate agent, mortgage person, hard money lender and contractor, your core real estate investing team is almost complete. The last core team member to add will be a tax advisor.

Why is the tax advisor last? Some new investors worry so much about saving money on taxes that they don't get started investing. They are so afraid of making a mistake and paying a few dollars more in taxes that they don't begin. It is a very big mistake because **you can't save money on taxes when you're not making any money.** A "tax write off" is worthless if there is no profits to write off. In order to incorporate tax saving strategies, you have to actually be making real money.

DISCLAIMER: I am not providing any tax advice.

You may want to consider spending far less time worrying about saving money on taxes early on and far more time on making money. With considerable profits coming in, you can then focus on how to best maximize your tax savings. And once you get to a level whereby you are making so much money that spending time and energy on tax savings can actually bring measurable results, you'll oftentimes find that a competent tax advisor may be one of your most valuable team members.

Finding a tax advisor that understands real estate investing can be challenging. Most CPAs and other tax professionals have very little knowledge of the tax laws that effect real estate investors. Ask other investors who they use and also ask your other team members, such as your real estate attorney. When you have the right tax person on your team, you can save far more in tax liability than the cost for the tax advisor's services.

Appendix B - Recommended Reading

I am often asked what I recommend investors read besides this book. Rising above the noise of hundreds of thousands of mediocre books, here are the top 5, in order, that I recommend to prospective real estate entrepreneurs. These 5 books you will want to read over and over again throughout your business and investing career. And as an added bonus, several of them are available for FREE at:
www.FreedomMentor.com/book

> **1. The Bible:** Surprised? Studies have shown that CEOs and business leaders the world over recognize the Bible as the #1 business book in their library. Specifically, read the book of Proverbs, 1 chapter each day (there are 31 chapters); it will take you a few minutes to complete each day. The author was King Solomon, the richest man in history. He knows a thing or two about success and money. You can get access to the Bible for free from several places. I recommend the YouVersion Bible app for your iPhone or Droid, but they also have an online version as well. YouVersion gives you access to several translations; I recommend the NIV 1984 translation. And further, I highly encourage you to seek the assistance of a mentor to help you fully comprehend the Bible (if you haven't already done so). It's the best selling book year after year and the best selling of all time for a reason.
>
> **2. Think and Grow Rich by Napolean Hill:** For over 75 years, this book has been the standard in inspiring people from all walks of life to achieve ex-

traordinary success and reach their goals. Many famous entrepreneurs credit this book as the spark that ignited their lifelong commitment to success. It is the original book on how to succeed and indeed the standard by which all other success books are measured. It has stood the test of time and is still the best personal development / success book available.

3. How to Win Friends and Influence People by Dale Carnegie: Real estate can be a people business. Knowing how to deal with people will make you a better investor. Dale Carnegie's classic, after 70 years, remains the standard in learning how to win friends and influence people. It has stood the test of time as well.

4. Awaken the Giant Within by Anthony Robbins: Real estate investors, as well as so many other self employed business owners and entrepreneurs, must learn how to take complete control over their actions and thoughts. The ability to take action and follow through is mandatory if you ever want to be successful in real estate. Tony Robbins is the foremost authority on helping people find their own personal power and awaken the giant within themselves. What Tony teaches are crucial skills you must have in order to reach your full potential on a daily basis and over a lifetime. Although other authors have communicated similar principles, Tony does an extraordinary job of simplifying complex concepts so that anyone can apply them to their lives.

5. Good to Great by Jim Collins: This is my personal favorite business book. It reveals the most productive way to build a very successful long term business. If you are going to be a real estate investor, it means you are going to be a business owner. Rather than read hundreds of business books, if you just read and apply what you learn from this one, you will be light years ahead of hundreds of thousands of businesses out there. Whether you are looking to build a one person operation or a huge company, the lessons you'll discover in this book are eye opening and incredibly powerful. Although this book hasn't been around as long as the others on this list, I believe that many years from now, Good to Great will be as popular and applicable as it is today. This book more than any other (except the Bible, of course), has had the most profound impact on my business life.

About the Author

Phil Pustejovsky is a best selling author, national speaker, accomplished investor and has been recognized as the leading coach and mentor in real estate. His works have been featured in CBS MoneyWatch, Wall Street Journal's MarketWatch and Yahoo! Finance. He frequently shares the stage with other legendary wealth experts such as Robert Kiyosaki, Robert Shemin and Peter Conti. Having been a part of more than 1,000 real estate investments himself, Phil is considered one of the most experienced investors alive. And for nearly a decade, Phil has been guiding everyday people to financial freedom though his innovative real estate investing techniques and strategies.

Connect with Phil

Google+:
http://plus.google.com/u/0/109060299146356821005
Facebook: http://www.facebook.com/philpustejovsky
YouTube: http://www.youtube.com/philpustejovsky
Twitter: http://www.twitter.com/philpustejovsky

Claim Your Free Bonuses

Don't forget to claim your free bonuses available to you because you purchased this book!

www.FreedomMentor.com/book

Made in the USA
Middletown, DE
11 July 2018